Infinite Music

Imaging the Next Millennium
of Human Music-Making

Infinite
Music

Imaging the Next Millennium
of Human Music-Making

Adam Harper

Winchester, UK
Washington, USA

First published by Zero Books, 2011
Zero Books is an imprint of John Hunt Publishing Ltd., Laurel House, Station Approach,
Alresford, Hants, SO24 9JH, UK
office1@o-books.net
www.o-books.com

For distributor details and how to order please visit the 'Ordering' section on our website.

Text copyright: Adam Harper 2010

ISBN: 978 1 84694 924 1

A CIP catalogue record for this book is available from the British Library.

Design: Stuart Davies

Printed in the UK by CPI Antony Rowe
Printed in the USA by Offset Paperback Mfrs, Inc

We operate a distinctive and ethical publishing philosophy in all
areas of our business, from our global network of authors to
production and worldwide distribution.

CONTENTS

For my grandfather, who insisted he was tone deaf.

Introduction: All Worlds

'To the makers of music – all worlds, all times'

– handwritten inscription on the Voyager Golden Record

There's a legend that sometime in the early nineteen-twenties Arnold Schoenberg, the Austrian composer regarded by many as the defining figure of musical modernism, proudly announced to his pupils Alban Berg and Anton Webern his discovery of a new compositional technique that would ensure the dominance of the German musical tradition for a thousand years. The technique was twelve-tone music, later called 'serialism', and it offered a method for the structuring of music to replace traditional tonality's system of keys – a harmonic convention Schoenberg had lead the way in superseding a decade before, inaugurating 'atonality'. The twelve-tone technique treated all twelve pitches in the Western octave equally, with each of them allotted an equal presence and significance within the musical work as part of a 'tone row' or 'series' that incorporated them all. In the subsequent decades the method developed into serialism and the same technique was applied to other musical variables such as duration, volume and timbre, becoming highly popular with composers in Europe and America. Today, serialism has all but died out, faith in musical modernism has subsided, and the legend seems more like a joke. There probably wasn't much truth in it to begin with, and it was most likely spread and embellished by some of Schoenberg's many detractors, wishing to draw parallels with the other declarations of lasting national dominance heard during that era.

When another leading modernist composer, Karlheinz Stockhausen, died at the end of 2007 another legend was told, this time among the composers based at the university music department where I was studying at the time. Apparently in the moments immediately before his death, Stockhausen had announced to onlookers his recent discovery of 'a new way of breathing' – after which he promptly collapsed. The joke was mean-spirited, but nonetheless betrayed a certain affection for a composer who'd probably done more to explore radical new musical worlds than any other, yet with little mainstream acceptance. The last movement of Schoenberg's Second String Quartet is often described as the very first example of atonality, and had featured a soprano ushering in musical modernism by singing the words: 'I feel air from other planets'.

Both of these stories thrive on the perceived failure of twentieth-century musical modernism. It's certainly difficult to argue that it came to enjoy as much public success as its protagonists and adherents would have liked it to. Of course, many people do appreciate and value this music, but these days much of this appreciation is found among small, often academic communities who, in spite of the ground-breaking efforts of their forebears, have almost paradoxically come to hold on to some very specific ideas about which particular forms of music and methods of composition are to be preferred, ignoring the growing diversity and complexity of the many other musical styles explored more freely by the wider public. Many focus on the historical facts of musical modernism such as atonality, apparently failing to recognise that music becomes modern relative to the conditions, perceptions and conventions of its time – modernism is not, in itself, a set of conventions. If music becomes conventional, it's by definition no longer modernist.

This book argues that musical modernism is not a state or a set of particular techniques or characteristics, but a direction. Modernism moves away from the strictures of tradition, progressively tearing them away piece by piece and leaving them behind as it travels towards an ultimately infinite potential for musical variety. In doing so it enhances the ways in which we perceive, imagine and live in the world. But there isn't just one, general and absolute path towards the infinite point of musical modernity, an assumption that came to stifle modernist music until it became, ironically, a new orthodoxy. Rather, each path is relative to a different starting point, a different context of convention. Modernism is a multi-directional and multi-dimensional process, and there are as many paths toward musical infinity as there are ways of composing and listening.

The musical modernists of the twenty-first century should follow the *spirit* of serialism and not its technique, its path of innovation and not its absolute solution, its difference and not its being repeated. Serialism sought to structure the entirety of music's wider (and ultimately infinite) possibilities with an even hand. This goal remains the same. But the sheer infinity of complex musical variety is too much to be squeezed into the discrete spans imposed on single musical works. Many serialist works aimed to have it all, all the time, an attitude that usually resulted in a structuring of musical variety so diffuse that it was difficult to perceive its workings in detail. Thus musical infinity had relatively little success at the level of the musical work itself. This made little difference, many of its adherents went on to claim, because the music was for experts and not meant for the general (or else somehow coerced) intelligences of the general public. So when interest in serialism subsequently all but died, it was assumed that this was because people – especially the general public – didn't really want music to be new and different, and that in a wider sense, radical attempts at innovation were hopeless, or at the most the exclusive preserve of a special minority cursed with the solitude of aesthetic superiority. What if this was an illusion, an overreaction?

What's more, serialism momentarily became the new orthodoxy because of its restrictions. Despite its noble aim to freely and equally structure the entire scope of musical variety, this variety was often permitted only for the single variable of pitch, or a limited range of the options expressed by other basic musical variables. Many serialist composers failed to perceive or challenge the even more fundamental conventions of their musical milieu: that the timbres they used were those of the instruments of Western classical music, centuries old, that the pitches and tunings they used were those of Western equal temperament and were even older. More fundamentally still, the music continued to be presented in the manner it had been for centuries: within a formal concert performance. Atonality was only one step on the road to musical modernity, and not its destination. The new musical possibilities that could be uncovered by the removal of still deeper conventions went unnoticed by many of the serialists. Other modernist composers, such as John Cage, Henry Cowell, Harry Partch and La Monte Young did travel beyond these conventions, but they didn't usually incorporate the egalitarianism of serialist techniques.

The greatest problem with serialism, though, was in its boiling down of all the complexity of music to one single, simple and absolute system of variables to be serialised, up to four in number: pitch, timbre, duration and volume. Pitch tended to take precedence, and to this day it's still seen as the most important, even the defining, variable in music. But music was nominally a construction of four variables and thus composition amounted to sculpture in a space of four dimensions. However, just as modernist music doesn't have one single set of characteristic techniques but operates instead relative to convention, so musical invention can't be reduced to four absolute dimensions, each constrained and finite. Technically, musical sound can be reduced even further to merely two dimensions: time and the amplitude of its sound wave. And these dimensions can be built up and combined in a number of ways to form more complex quantities that composers may wish to observe and control, such as timbres, harmonies, rhythms, melodies and any structure there may not yet be a name for. So where do we draw a line around what musical variables composers should observe and potentially serialise?

We don't. That was the old serialism, the old modernism. There can be no one absolute foundation for music. And there can be no prior assumptions, no prior techniques and conventions – no restrictions whatsoever. We can't even assume any ultimate distinction between musical activity and the wider lives of ourselves and the universe. That's what the meaning of musical infinity is, and it's in that direction that any future modernist endeavour must travel. Infinite music necessitates an *n-dimensional modernism*. Its egalitarian serialisation – in individual musical works or among a group of works – can approach infinity, increasing in scope and richness as it goes, but will never actually reach it, and so modernism can only ever amount to a relative direction rather than a fixed state. Serialism and modernism are dead. Long may they live.

Modernity is the challenge of the infinite within the capacities of the present. Musical modernists seek to maximise the possibilities of composition to the utmost degree, taking in equally both its broad and deep possibilities and those at the finest levels of detail (composers regularly lose themselves between these two extremes, ignoring or unaware of the entire range). This infinity of possible permutations in musical variety has often been a topic of discussion. In 1959 the composer and conductor Leonard Bernstein gave a television lecture entitled 'The Infinite Variety of Music', concerned with, as its title suggests, the richness of musical variation.[1] To illustrate this, Bernstein took a simple sequence of four pitches and gave a number of examples of how that sequence had been varied across different examples of (mainly Western classical) music. In a preamble he noted that the number of other possible combinations of pitches stretched to a number that was over a hundred digits long. With chords (i.e. more than one pitch sounding simultaneously) taken into account, this number increases to over three hundred digits. Of course, not only did this just describe the numerical potential of one variable – pitch – but it only took into account the twelve pitches of the Western classical system.

With the much finer possibilities and control over musical variables offered by recently developed and increasingly accessible electronic music technology, this number truly explodes. Since the nineteen-fifties (the heyday of Bernstein and musical modernism) countless musical performances have occurred and musical variables invented, used and perceived that cannot be counted within Bernstein's number. Many of these came from an arena of music-making some still call 'popular music' – the term is quaint, in many ways incorrect, in some contexts has an offensive tinge, and will probably lose its currency over the next century. 'Popular music' can either mean 'music that is widely appreciated' or else music *for* 'the people' or *by* 'the people', regardless of how many people actually appreciate it. I'm referring to the third category, but either way the term is generally a catch-all category for music that isn't thought to be Western classical music. Since the Second World War this 'popular music' has been increasing exponentially in diversity and complexity, incorporating new, technological structures and forms and becoming a powerful new site for musical modernism.

It hopefully goes without saying, then, that modernist music isn't limited to one particular musical style or genre, but can and will manifest through hundreds and thousands of different styles. In any case, the main thrust of musical modernism has largely fallen out of the hands of Western classical music over the last fifty years. In its current state, it rarely offers those hungry for the musically new anything more than convention upon convention – a long, deep and undeniably rich tradition that Schoenberg never escaped from. These conventions are sonic, but in the end they are deeper still: the concert, the concert hall, the smartly dressed musicians playing age-old instruments of wire, wood and brass, the silenced audience. Too often, the elitism is social as well as artistic. Western classical music – we could call it 'non-popular music' – has long ceased to assume a place of absolute privilege and priority in musical culture as a whole. It's given and may well continue to give us some of those works of art our culture has appreciated the most, but today its general tendency towards myopic traditionalism and exclusivity makes it tiny against the enormous backdrop of infinite musical possibility, which is calling more loudly than ever before.

A number of the cultural assumptions we make about music and musical concepts live on, however, inherited from centuries of Western classical music and its aesthetic ideologies. A 'composer', for example, is routinely held to be a specially trained person (usually a man) who writes music using Western classical notation, which is then given to an ensemble of specially trained musicians playing Western classical instruments. But technically the word 'composer' suggests anyone at all who might create music. In this sense, the term overlaps with the word 'performer'. Composers may also come in groups that collaborate on the creation of music. In this book I retain the word 'composer' because of this fundamental meaning, but in no way should it be assumed that I am talking about classical music, or classical music composers, or composers who write for live or acoustic instruments, or specially trained or professional artists. No, with the word 'composer' I'll be referring to *any source of music at all*, multiple or otherwise, including performers (be they singers or instrumentalists), producers, singer-songwriters, 'artists', sound artists, DJs and other selectors, artificial sources and even, in a significant sense, people who play music to themselves alone, with an instrument or the press of a button. We can all be composers, and we are all composers. This must not be forgotten as you read. Nor does the term imply any particular value or privileged position – all these figures are equal. To emphasise all of this, I've only used the word in plural form.

Similarly, when I talk of the possibilities of 'music', I don't prioritise or 'really mean' classical music, as the term is often used in certain circles. Nor do I 'really mean' any sort of popular or Western music. I don't even 'really mean' 'art' music, or 'difficult' music, or 'serious' music – awkward terms that have been used to differentiate, separate and territorialise musical activity in the past. I don't even mean whatever we consider to be 'good' music. I mean music in all its senses, all its past, present and future senses. Music in senses that haven't even been discovered or practiced yet. Music before categories and without prejudices, to the fullest possible extent of the word's meanings and consequences.[2]

How can music be infinite in such a way? Its possibilities can't literally become actualised as infinite, of course, as long as the various systems that perform music are somehow finite, which will necessarily be the case since the universe itself is physically constrained. For this reason we should consider these possibilities *virtually* infinite. Besides which, an infinite variety of music isn't necessarily desirable in itself. Even with the best intentions it can't be denied that we appreciate some permutations of musical possibility more than others, depending on context, and that our capacity to appreciate music has some relation to the prior musical systems we've become familiar with. Does musical modernism fail to take this into account? Only partially – if modernism is a directional process, the music it creates is always somewhere *between* the old and familiar and the indiscriminate infinity of different forms, proceeding only *toward* the latter. It's a relation between old and new, and any given moment of modernist music will present a mixture of what can be appreciable to a given audience to any extent as either old or new. So not only must modernism reject any one absolute system, path or final resting place, but it must also situate itself with respect to the familiar in some way, however small, and this link with or establishment of the familiar is what can facilitate appreciation.

Here, perhaps, is a way to bringing more listeners to modernist music than it won in the twentieth century.

But why all this talk of modernism and infinity? Why does music need to align itself with the maximum compositional possibilities of its time? Aren't things just fine the way they are? Why write this book? The issue is one of *imagination*. Music is one of the activities that can stoke it, and not just in some abstract, exclusively artistic sense. There is no absolute border between the musical imagination and the imagination of anything else in life. The widening of an imagination to accommodate a new and unusual idea or possibility can be a rewarding experience in itself, but this process is also the engine of our development and betterment as individuals and as societies. Sometimes ideas become difficult to imagine; often we can't tell when our imaginations have become limited and we can no longer detect what might lie beyond their horizons, making us ignorant both of the way things really are and the way things might one day be.

I would argue that music, both in its composition and in its appreciation (not entirely differentiable categories, as we'll see), often faces such a predicament and is actually facing one today. For many people it's difficult to imagine the future of music as being anything very different to what it is at present. This is compounded by the notion that in the last century we've supposedly learned the lesson that radical musical innovation along the lines of serialism will only be unsuccessful. We might even lapse into an attitude of some cruel irony concerning matters of glittering, confident musical futures, an irony by turns tragic or mocking: the jokes – Schoenberg, Stockhausen – receive their punch-lines. Or else we ignore it, or remain ignorant entirely. Either way we've perpetuated the status quo.

Why shouldn't we try to imagine another thousand years of musical history? Why shouldn't we try to feel the air of other planets? Is stagnation and comfortable, unwitting boredom preferable? Twentieth-century musical modernism may appear to have ended in failure when compared to its loftiest ambitions, but the future of the human musical imagination is about more than the rehabilitation of that same old twentieth-century modernism. This enters a far deeper current of human history. We could say that musical modernism is a process that also occurred at other moments in music history that may not be as well-known today, but had huge repercussions for the increasing richness of music: bass-led harmony and opera (in the seventeenth century), the precise division of musical time (in the fourteenth century), even polyphony and tuning itself are the products of musical innovation – of venturing into a detailed musical infinity – down the ages, and that's only Western music.

This book proposes a system for the imagining of music. It's not just a single system as was offered by serialism, but a system of systems, an infinite system allowing for the creation of subordinate musical systems or what will be called 'musical objects', describing how they interrelate and how they're perceived (or not). It sees music as a *complex system of variables relating primarily to the production of sound*, and takes this idea to its infinitely variable conclusions. This system, which is given the name 'music space', situates the limitations of any one, particular idea or set of ideas about musical forms against a space of infinite variability expressed in infinite dimensions. It ultimately treats all music as *a process of continuously changing information* and thus at the point of infinity, music, which manifests as an event, is always unrepeatable and different (i.e. changed) unless we restrict the perception of this change in some way. We see every musical structure as one of different relative rates of this change, with some elements changing while others repeat or remain effectively the same. We see how the same structures of musical change apply both within and outside of the borders of musical performances, making music as a whole a single system spanning all lengths of time. We see how composers and listeners perceive this change in relation to their own capacities and interests and thus come to handle and develop musical information discriminately. Most importantly, by imagining music in terms of paths of possible change running through a space of infinite possibility, we learn how the restrictions of unwitting convention and the apparent finitude of our imaginations can be detected and thus overcome.

This book is for both for composers (meaning anyone who creates music) and listeners. It assumes very little prior familiarity with the various technical terms and concepts in music – instead, it offers a new vocabulary. Examples and analogies are given where possible, but it'll naturally be a challenge to express complex musical structures that haven't yet been invented as musical concepts, so we generally have to make do with the usual typological landscape of musical works, instruments, styles, notes, sounds, melodies and so on. The infinite world beyond them is given its space, but has to remain largely undemonstrated and should always be borne in mind. The system presented here also draws influence from areas of contemporary philosophy, musicology, psychology, statistics, geometry, physics, information theory and speculative astrobiology but again, the concepts involved are for the most part explained and framed afresh rather than reliant on much prior familiarity with, reference to, or quotation and transplanted terminology from these discourses.

Each part of this book expresses broadly the same set of ideas, with each adding its own successive layer of conceptual detail in framing these ideas. Part 1 is an introduction to the concept of musical variables and how they operate and combine to form structures. Along the way we'll define music and its relationship to wider life, and see it as something that changes, most notably at the point of performance. Part 2 is a more technical exploration of the matters arising from Part 1, examining the properties and development of 'musical objects' within music space and the nature of musical information, how it can increase and decrease. This leads to an understanding of musical experimentation and imagination, and to an ethos of composition. Part 3 deals with the aesthetics or perception of music, noting that listening to music is an active, interested and discriminatory process dependent on our capacities and needs. Listening and aestheticising turns musical objects into 'images of music' whose limitations can hinder more imaginative listening. Part 3 consequently arrives at a definition of musical modernism as pertaining relative to these images, and concludes by positing three successive categories of invention in new music.

Written ten years into a new millennium that has already seen widespread and significant technological change as well as scientific discovery, this book is not primarily a guide to what will happen in the next thousand years of human music-making (if we survive that long), although it does make a few predictions and suggestions, and its system is designed to encompass all possible musical change that may arise in that time. The word 'millennium' doesn't just refer to a period of a thousand years, either, but also suggests a new era, one with generally positive connotations. My hope – barefacedly idealistic enough to rival those of the modernists of precisely a century ago – is that it will see the virtually infinite possibilities of music more easily accessed by humanity as a whole. If nothing else, this is at least a goal for modernist music.

Why *human* music-making? Are there other kinds of music-making? Perhaps – but here, 'human' is intended not so much as a qualification for or an all-too-tragic limitation on musical possibility than as an invitation to it. Humanity doesn't equate to a set of given biological, evolutionary or social constraints, but is constantly adapting and developing from the old, familiar and limited humanity to new forms of humanity, using tools and technology and increasing its capacity for imagination and information as it does so. Music goes along with it, as a part of this process.

The scope and achievement of human music-making to date regularly goes unappreciated. I'm not only referring to the well-known canonical gravitas of figures like Bach and Beethoven, but to the broader variety of the world's musical culture and its wide array of detailed approaches. Speaking of humanity's capacity to use tools and technology to gather new information and ultimately reach the infinite, a representatively diverse compilation of recorded human music known as the Voyager Golden Record was attached to each of the two Voyager space probes, launched in 1977. Having photographed the planets and moons of the outer solar system, Voyager 1 is now rapidly heading out of our solar system and has by some distance become the farthest human-made object from Earth, roughly ten billion miles away at the current time of writing. Inspiringly Romantic as this is, the Golden Record also reveals just some of the rich possibilities of human music-making that have already been realised. They were selected by a committee chaired by astronomer and cosmologist Carl Sagan and include examples from four centuries of the Western classical concert tradition (Bach and Beethoven make five appearances between them) as well as musical styles from India, Africa, China, South and North America, Southeast Asia, Eastern Europe and Oceania. Complementing the outer areas of musical possibility sketched by the modernist composers of the mid-twentieth century, the record demonstrates the depth of complexity that can come to fill this broad space – then, now and in the future.

The Golden Record is intended as an emissary of the mid-twentieth-century human race, on the off-chance that any extraterrestrial life-forms (or future humans) recover it. Even if it is weighted towards Western music, compiled by Western ears and doesn't take in the experimental and electronic music developed in the second half of the twentieth century (and particularly towards its end, after launch), its complexity and diversity is still deeply instructive. With music heading all the time into new territories, sometimes rapidly, sometimes more slowly, what would an equivalent of the Voyager Golden Record sound like in a thousand years' time? Would Bach and Beethoven still seem significant enough within the archives of human musical achievement to merit an appearance, or will they, like the monastic chant of the first millennium AD previously that doesn't appear on the Golden Record, be deemed too obscure, not rich enough compared with the more recent millennium's achievements? Voyager 1 is scheduled to pass within 1.6 light years of the star AC+79 3888 in forty thousand years; what will human music be like then? What, if anything, will be the capacity and meaning of the categories 'human' and 'music'? What would any space-faring future humans or extraterrestrial life-forms make of it if it were found? The chances seem remote – the probe, with all its wealth of musical information, is nonetheless a very tiny object set against the enormous backdrop of the space it's travelling through. Or to reverse the scenario, what will Voyager 1, leaving the familiarity of Earth at a speed of roughly seventeen kilometres a second, find if it ever meets something? What would an extraterrestrial equivalent of the Voyager Golden Record sound like? And couldn't the music of future humans have become just as alien during Voyager's journey?

How will we come to compose and recognise this music of the future? By seeing it in terms of its most fundamental condition: change itself.

Part 1: Musical Variables

In order to compose music, we should ask what it is that music is composed of. We need to know what building materials we have to hand for the creation of new musical structures, how they work and how they can be combined. Furthermore, if we want to maximise the possibilities of composition to the utmost degree we need to be aware of what the most fundamental levels of composition consist of, what the smallest possible units, the building blocks, of compositional choice are. By analogy, if we wanted to truly maximise the possibilities of architecture it wouldn't be enough to conclude that the smallest possible unit involved in building, say, a house is the brick, even if bricks can be used to form an enormous number of different structures. We'd have to go beyond the level of bricks to a much smaller, deeper scale, beyond plaster, concrete, glass and steel, even. If the technology permitted it, we'd want to be able to build houses on the level of a much more radical, fundamental condition of creation – by manipulating forces at the subatomic level.

How do we reach such a point in musical composition? To draw a parallel with the bricks in architecture example, it's too simplistic, too limited, to say that music is fundamentally composed of musical notes. It may seem like common sense to describe a musical work as a collection of individual but connected notes of different pitches and lengths (an idea that has a long history) but such a description doesn't allow for sounds that can't be reduced to what we conventionally handle as notes. All the details involved in a voice singing a melody, with all the subtle quality of intonation and timing this entails, can't be boiled down to 'notes' as we conventionally know them. At the most, notes are merely the written starting point for certain types of singers, the outline within which a complex and unique performance will occur.

Naturally this depends to varying degrees on the kind of notation used, and whether the notation is used as a performing instruction or as a transcription for the purposes of listening along. It's not difficult to see, though, that the most common system, Western classical notation – of crotchets, quavers, staves, clefs, notes of an octave A through G and so on – is insufficient to describe most of the sounds that can be created in much practical detail or at a level of detail we may wish to express. These may be sounds we might want to incorporate into music, and modern music technology makes it much easier for us to do this. Such sounds – *sounds beyond notes* – have always been an important part of music, even if the dominating influence of Western classical notation has made it easy for us to forget this, rendering us less aware of them and disinclined to use them with detail. Sounds beyond notes are especially important now, in the age of recording and electronic music, when sound is being manipulated in ways that previous generations of composers and listeners were probably unable even to imagine.

We might say that music is fundamentally composed of *sound* or *sounds*, then, and this seems perfectly adequate. Think a bit further, though, and it seems a little vague for our purposes. Are there many sounds or one sound in a piece of music? How should we finally divide music into its particular constituent sounds, or reassemble it out of these constituent parts? Where might one sound begin and another end – are there sounds within sounds? What about silence? In what specific ways can we constitute sounds? Are sounds static or do they change – could we say that a sound can change from one sound into another sound? Might there be more to music than sound? We may rarely run into problems talking about 'this sound' or 'that sound' in everyday life, but when it comes to composing music, the nature and potential of sounds and their free combination makes isolating the category of *individual* sounds more complex. Most importantly, if we can manipulate sounds in many ways so that they can be and become anything at all – long or short, high or low, loud or quiet – then simply settling on a category of 'sounds' doesn't have much use or tangibility as a fundamental creative condition of composition. We might as well be philosophers or scientists concluding that the world consists of 'things', and leaving it at that.

Paths of Change

To find a more useful fundamental creative condition of composition, we'd need a way of expressing that power to manipulate sound by grasping the specific attributes of any sound based on the ways in which it varies. There is a term for this, common in maths, science and their applications: *variables*. The Cambridge Dictionary of Statistics describes a variable as 'some characteristic that differs from subject to subject or from time to time'.[3] Another dictionary is slightly more specific but no more or less correct, defining a variable as 'a quantity or characteristic that can take on different values'.[4] By way of a summary definition, we could say that a variable describes one single way in which the attributes of something can vary, and that variation is a variation in measurable *values*.

'Height', 'weight', 'eye colour', 'age' and 'shoe size' are just some of the variables that can be used to describe certain attributes of people, for example. The values given by these variables, that is, the attributes of specific people, are measured in different ways (respectively: metres, kilograms, words denoting colours and so on) and will change from person to person. Variables can be thought of as the 'settings' of things, as on an electrical appliance. In much the same way that a television is 'set to' a certain channel and a certain volume, brightness (etc.) the height variable of some people is currently 'set to' five feet and ten inches, in other people it's 'set to' six feet and two inches, while other people have other heights and so on. As well as changing from person to person, the values given by the variables of height and weight will change over time, within the lifespan of a single person.

We can call variables that may be applied to music *musical variables*. Each one describes a way in which the attributes of music can vary. Each one represents a single choice of 'setting', a single area, path or *locus* of possible control and specification that may be available to the composers in manipulating the music – we can simply imagine the words 'what' or 'which' in front of a word describing the variable to imagine the compositional choice that a variable creates ('at what volume', 'which pitch' etc.). A musical variable together with a value appropriate to it constitutes one piece of information about some music. Most pieces of music (or *musical works*, as I'll be calling them) could be described as sets of fixed or changeable values given by hundreds of different kinds of musical variables, if not more. Each one describes something, whether it be the tiniest details of a single individual note's precise pitch or length, say, or the ranges or other attributes of whole melodies, rhythms, harmonies, instruments and ultimately all musical structures, of every type and at every scale. As we'll see, musical variables may also operate outside the bounds of what we conventionally consider to be pieces of music.

Common, basic musical variables include volume, pitch and timbre.[5] Time can also be expressed by musical variables, both as a measure of the *durations* of individual sounds or other musical structures as well as the *positions* of sounds or other musical structures within other time continuums, that is, other durations. Because of the tendency, originating in part from the traditions of Western classical music, to think of music in terms of pitched notes, these variables are often conventionally assumed be more or less the only basic choices available to the composers regarding individual sounds. Far from it. There are many more musical variables that one can consider, particularly with the finer and more complex control enabled by the music production technology of the last fifty years. Using certain devices that process electrical sound signals, composers can vary the amount and quality of distortion ('crackliness' or 'noisiness', to put it crudely) a sound has, for example, while low-pass filtration allows composers to control how 'muffled' a sound can be. In some styles of music, such as noise music, the attention given to the manipulation of these variables is on an equal, perhaps even higher footing than those of pitch, duration and timbre when it comes to the way the music is composed and appreciated. There's no reason to think them somehow inherently subordinate or secondary to more traditional musical variables.

Sound-manipulating machines like those that create distortion and filtration are often called 'effects', and they can manifest as either hardware or software. They themselves can be controlled with a number of 'settings' or variables. Take a reverberation or 'reverb' effect, for example. Reverb is what you hear as a sound dies away within a large space enclosed with surfaces that reflect sound, such as a cathedral. You don't need electric signal-processing effects to make reverb a deliberately controlled attribute within a musical composition (composers such as Pauline Oliveros have made music using natural reverb, for example), but particularly when using a device like a computer, composers can control a large number of variables that describe some more specific attributes of the reverb. These may include the length of time the sound takes to die away, the amount of the signal that is processed by the reverb, the size of the simulated 'room' creating the reverb, how the reverb mixes with itself, the relative volume of the reverb and so on.[6] Or the composers may choose to keep things simple, and only concern themselves with some of the variables that can describe reverb, and leave the rest to software defaults or some pre-established ('preset') settings. In this case the most basic variable describing reverb is a *binary variable*, that of whether the reverb is switched on or off. So variables can describe both the minute, highly specific and complex details of music and the very basic and vastly consequential characteristics of it, and they can operate on any and every level of the compositional process. Composers may observe and use as many or as few variables as they like, with the effect of the variables on their music becoming as complex or as simple as they choose.

But if musical variables can be everything between 'very basic' or 'vastly consequential', then doesn't this make them a rather strange 'fundamental condition of composition'? Normally when we think of fundamental levels of creation, we think of constituent objects like atoms, electrons or quarks, but this isn't the case with music, which can't easily or ultimately be reduced to single tiny building blocks in this way. Musical variables are a different sort of fundamental condition of creation, in that they're able to express music not as composed of certain static building blocks (such as 'notes' or 'sounds'), but as particular paths taken by *musical change* – the changing values that make up musical information – itself. And any change whatsoever in music, however big or small, can theoretically be described by the variation of a single, notional variable, a single locus or path of change, 'as the crow flies'. If we suppose that music can be described as continuously changing information, then there can be no more fundamental a unit of that change than the musical variable itself.

So far I've only been discussing variables that describe the attributes of sounds, but musical variables can also describe the *interrelationships* between sounds or other variables. These may describe the distance or difference between sounds across the span of other variables such as pitch (i.e. the gap or 'interval' between two pitches, which is a factor of harmony) or across time (which is a factor that goes into the creation of rhythms). Again, variables like 'difference in distortion', or 'difference in reverb' aren't widely used or held to matter in most music, but thinking of variability in this way helps us to imagine kinds of music in which they could.

Variables can also describe what, when and how sounds and other musical structures are repeated. They can even control the values and general operation of other variables. In musical works that allow for different outcomes from performance to performance (or *at the point of performance*), the values given by one variable or set of variables could depend in some way on the values of another variable that changes in some way. This changeability may be due to other circumstances, or the choice of performers, or because they're random every time. In this case, variables would be interrelated as *independent* and *dependent* variables in a system that only gives rise to certain controlled outcomes.

Let's imagine a simple example: some composers could create a musical work for two performers, giving the instruction that if Performer A is (for whatever reason beyond the composers' direct specification) making a high-pitched sound, then Performer B must make a low-pitched sound, perhaps so as to balance pitch within the system. Here, the values given one pitch variable (at Performer A) – the independent variable – would determine the values given by another pitch variable (at Performer B) – the dependent variable. Roughly speaking, the relationship between those values is one of inverse proportion. Or their interrelationship could be reciprocal, with both Performer A and Performer B equally listening to each other constantly so that if one is high, the other is low and vice versa.

There are many sorts of improvised music, such as Central African polyphony or compositions by avant-garde composers such as John Zorn, in which sounds or parts of the music are arranged in a much more complex web of dependent and independent interrelationships, all described by the activity of variables and their values. Making music like this is more like playing a game such as football, with players observing rules concerning the activity of variables and reaching different outcomes, than a musical work in the most traditional sense. There would be little point in recording such music for the purposes of repeated listening, because the idea is that every game is different. Participating or observing this game-like music-making, provided you had some knowledge of the rules, would be the best way to experience it. In Central African 'pygmy' polyphony, for example, rather than amounting to a fixed sequence of notes with a fixed rhythm (as it conventionally would be in Western music) each 'song' is a loose pattern of favoured intervals and rhythms together with complex rules for how improvisation may deviate from them, and how the improvisation is divided among the singers of the group.

'Building Up' and 'Breaking Down' Musical Variables

One example of an important variable describing an interrelationship between sounds is that of 'texture'. This term refers to the shape formed by a collection of sounds regarding their pitches, durations and positions in time relative to one another. Texture can be thought of as the 'silhouette' of music or a part of it, and in this respect it's visualised on the piano roll of a player piano as the sound-causing indentations distributed across the 'silent', non-indented, two-dimensional backdrop of the roll. Some of the technical terms used to describe textures include 'homophonic', (different sounds starting and finishing at the same time, as in a harmonised hymn), 'polyphonic' (many 'voices' producing sound at different pitches and rhythms, as in a fugue – though a fugal texture can be seen as a specific kind of polyphonic texture), 'monophonic' (a single voice only, as in solo monastic chant) or 'in contrary motion' (where the texture is largely symmetrical across an axis given by a certain pitch), but a texture can also be more casually described as 'sparse', 'fragmented', 'tight-knit' and so on. These words can correspond to the values with which the variable of texture is measured.

The variable of texture, then, is a variable that has the

behaviour of more basic, 'smaller' variables of pitch (or interval), time position (or interrelated distances over time) and sound duration incorporated or implicated 'within it'. It implies the interrelationship of many different variables as it describes certain sorts of interrelationships between sounds along the path of a single variable. Or to put it another way, the variable of texture's values can be given as or 'broken down' into variables and values of pitch, time position and sound duration and the relationships between them. As with reverb, issues of texture can be controlled through the fine-tuning of individual pitch and rhythm variables, or we could think of a texture variable as simply presenting a choice between an array of pre-existing ('preset') structures – a homophonic texture, a polyphonic texture, a monophonic texture and so on.

The way texture can be 'broken down' into variables shows us the process by which musical variables and the values they give combine and work together, 'building up' to form larger structures within music. In turn, these structures may be handled as values (or ranges of values) given by composite yet singular variables, with single paths of change that vary musical attributes in a unified motion. Texture is one of the attributes of music that implicates other, 'smaller' attributes, but it can still be treated as a single variable by composers and listeners. Similarly, structures of many variables may work together to themselves become values expressed by new variables. These could be variables that (unlike texture) haven't yet been discovered and do not have names and definitions, but which could conceivably play an important role in musical change. Understanding music as a collection of musical variables and their interrelationships enables us to imagine such structures.

Eventually, the activity of thousands of variables and their values (potentially more) can be seen to work together to describe every aspect of the attributes of a musical work and the changes those attributes may go through in the length of time the music occupies. During the composition of a musical work many of the decisions made involving these variables aren't in themselves even consciously considered by composers. Normally composers operate through specific channels as they make music and handle specific groups of variables, but ultimately variables and the interrelationships between them are behind every conceivable decision composers make, and at every stage of composition. I'm not suggesting that composers should pay attention to every single possible musical variable as they compose (though they can try if they like), but thinking of music as a complex system of variables does reveal more clearly the full potential of music's *variability* – its potential to differ – whichever variables composers do or don't choose to keep in mind during specific instances of music-making.

Music Before Sounds

Up to this point, for the sake of simplicity, I've talked about variables as *describing* the attributes of individual 'sounds' and the interrelationships between them. In fact, it's obvious that when it comes to musical composition, sounds don't exist independently of the activity of the variables and values that specify them. Sounds are made up of values expressed by variables, whatever they may be: it's the activity of combinations of variables and their values that actually *creates* or *constitutes* in the first place what we may then identify as (certain) sounds. There's no such thing as a sound without values, that is, values that can be expressed through variables. For composers, variables can do more than just describe sound(s) – they are in a significant sense what compose them.

This is one of the key reasons why I suggested earlier that 'sounds' were too vague and insufficient a basis for the fundamental creative conditions of composition. Musical variability comes *before* sounds, not vice versa. Besides which, musical variables can create far more than what we conventionally consider to be 'sounds'. In themselves, rhythms, textures and harmonies are not conventionally thought of as individual 'sounds', and yet they're comprised of variables. They're concepts that describe ways of ordering sound(s) perhaps, but pure rhythm creates no sound in itself without a variable of timbre being assigned a value – and yet thinking of pure rhythm, independently of timbre, pitch or any other variables, can be of huge importance to composers. For example, I could reproduce the same rhythm on a drum, or a horn, or a desk, or on many different instruments with or without pitch variables, and I may well use different pitches on the notes of the rhythm each time. In this case, we wouldn't normally call that rhythm *itself* a sound because it can manifest through a range of timbres and pitches. The same applies to any other structure in music-making, structures we would have difficulty referring to by that crude term 'sounds'.

Linked to this is another problem I've alluded to, that of whether we can isolate these 'sounds' as having a singular, autonomous, indivisible existence, bearing in mind that we want to be able to vary sound as much as we possibly can, creating an infinitude of forms at any scale. When multiple sounds and attributes are interrelated, especially if they occur simultaneously or close together across a variable such as time or pitch, they can be said to combine and become other, 'bigger' or 'higher' sounds or sonic structures, which in turn go to make up the 'single sound' that we might call a piece of music. It works the other way, too: take 'one sound' and it can usually be described as an aggregation of smaller sounds or sonic structures and silences, right down to the point of the vibrating of atoms and molecules in the air (or whatever else) that serves as the medium for sound waves. There isn't a single absolute sense in which we can isolate what we normally think of as a single sound – we can conceivably describe any single sound as being composed of a multiplicity of smaller sounds, or as a constituent part of a larger sound. Naturally, we can put up potentially arbitrary conceptual borders for the sake of convention and functionality that tell us what *certain* sounds are to relatively limited degrees of specificity, but as we're dealing with the maximum possibilities of musical form here, such categorical borders will melt away. These borders are an illusion that limits the way we imagine music's variability as a continuous whole that applies prior to specific, individual categories.

Since 'sounds' ultimately become difficult to pin down as coherent, singular musical entities, it's easier and more constructive to describe music fundamentally in terms of variables, in terms of changing attributes and 'settings', rather than individual 'sounds' as such. Far better for composers, then, to concern themselves with music's variability itself, the ever-changing attributes of sound, and not the slippery being of 'sounds themselves'. Manipulate the variables, and the resulting sounds will take care of themselves: they'll arise through the perception of composers and listeners by means music's fundamental variability, rather than from a certain collection of static sounds that somehow exist prior to music and *then* become subject to variability.

That *music comes before sounds* in this way may not seem intuitively obvious. This may be because differentiating and isolating what unproblematically appear to be individual sounds rarely becomes a practical problem in everyday life, and because most conventional music is generally based on patterns of clear, relatively autonomous and differentiable notes, phrases and sound samples. In the last century particularly, however, much music has been written that challenges a listener's ability to straightforwardly discern or isolate individual, singular sounds within the music (which is by no means a necessary criterion for good musical composition). This is much like how an abstract or semi-abstract picture might challenge a viewer's ability to discern or isolate and recognise discrete objects, whether they're previously familiar to the viewer or not.

At this point we need to deal with a problem. If sounds can become anything at all by virtue of their changing attributes and the interrelationships between them, then it follows that unfeasibly large numbers of variables can be said to apply within a single musical work or a part thereof. If the relationships between any two virtually infinitesimal areas within the music can conceivably be specified through a variable, then the number of variables that can be used to describe a musical work could be virtually infinite. However, this isn't a problem for composers, who freely choose which relationships to control within the music, that is, which variables are relevant during composition. On the contrary – composers are fortunate in having a virtually infinite field of choice over which variables to observe.

This may become a problem for musical analysts in the field of musicology, though, and similarly, but to a lesser extent, listeners (who don't need to be as objective or scholarly). It's the task of the analyst and the listener to effectively 'de-compose' a musical work by observing the activity of any variables, finding the more important areas of variability, and accordingly dividing or differentiating the resulting sound(s) up into relevant sections and symbols and the relevant interrelationships between them as they perceive it. For example, the relationship between the first two notes of a musical work may become more important to a listener, and so perhaps more relevant to an analysis, than that of two other notes chosen at random from within the entire work, even though both relationships between both sets of notes could be determined by variables. Since our topic is the infinite possibilities of composition, where we are free to choose, manipulate and specify variables as much or as little as we like, and not a guide to how a musical analyst might usefully tackle music's potentially infinite variability, these problems needn't concern us for now.

Specifying Variables within a Musical Context, or 'Taking Variables into Account'

By now I hope it's becoming clear that there are huge numbers of variables that composers may use as they create music, especially when it comes to modern recording technology. Anyone familiar with digital audio software such as Ableton Live, Logic or Pro Tools can appreciate how many thousands of individual musical variables can be brought into the composition of music today. Even a relatively basic software synthesiser allows its user to control dozens of variables: pitch, volume and duration, obviously, but also timbre through the type of waveform with which the synthesiser creates its oscillating signal. The user can also specify the precise tuning of the synthesiser often to the hundredth of a semitone, how many oscillators (or voices) sound each time a note is pressed, how long a note takes to reach its full volume, pitch or frequency when a note is pressed and how long the note takes to die away after the note is released. As well as all this, low frequency oscillators may be activated, which can control how quickly, how drastically and in what shape the notes will oscillate in pitch, frequency or filtration as they're held.

Of course, many of these variables can apply to traditional acoustic instruments too, but here's the difference: not all of them are *taken into account* within the context of certain stylistic conventions and/or the musical notation they use. In contrast to the modern synthesiser with its enhanced possibilities, most classical composers today (and throughout history) don't concern themselves with specifying the very precise tunings in their music. It's taken for granted that when the musical instructions (i.e. the score) are followed by the performer, the performer will already have made sure that they are tuned according to whatever tuning conventions they observe. Classical acoustic performers also regularly use what amounts to an equivalent of the synthesiser's 'low frequency oscillator' when they play, oscillating rapidly in pitch by small amounts in a technique known as *vibrato*. Again, classical composers almost never specify any of the values for variables that could describe this vibrato in the musical score, as it's a matter left to the performer. So modern synthesisers allow more areas of control over sound – that is to say, they take more variables into account – than previous generations of composers took into account. This high level of control and sonic specification has become very important in a lot of recent electronic music, where extremely subtle use of timbre, tuning and rhythm has come to carry considerable aesthetic weight. Indeed, effective usage of these subtle new possibilities can be seen as a new standard of musical modernity.

This notion of 'taking variables into account' when thinking about music within a certain context can be quite revealing. In a given musical context, such as a style or a wider tradition of music, we can ask ourselves what musical variables are or aren't taken into account when it comes to composition or performance, either due to technology (as in the case of distortion, which requires an electrical device and so wasn't taken into account before electric instruments were invented) or merely due to convention (as in the case of precise tuning, which most composers didn't conventionally specify). Before we go any further, then, since we are looking to maximise the possibilities of musical composition: are there any potentially significant types of variables that are conventionally left out – *discounted* – when thinking about or composing music in the Western tradition?

Music After Sounds: Non-sonic Variables

I would argue that there's a major group of potentially musical variables routinely thought not be a part of music, or the so-called 'music itself'. These are *non-sonic variables*, and they describe any attribute or circumstance of music that is not, or is not exclusively, to do with sound. Basic non-sonic variables would detail *who* or *what* produces the music or parts of it, and *when*, *where* and *how* it's produced. They can also be more detailed, concerning aspects such as dress, climate, mood, use of physical movement by performers or audience, use of a demarcated performance area, use of spoken or written commentary (from something like 'this is a song we wrote while touring in Iceland' uttered on stage by a lead singer all the way to CD liner notes) and presentation in general. Even something like whether or not the music is dedicated to someone or something, which may lead to a further variable, who or what the music is dedicated to, is worth considering as part of the music, as it is in fact a compositional choice that will affect the way we experience the music just as other more traditional musical variables do. The title of a musical work could be considered an example of a non-sonic variable that is, in many respects, unknowingly taken into account.

The outcomes of some variables can be thought of as partly sonic and partly non-sonic – for example, if some composers were to deliberately specify that a work should be performed in a cathedral using a variable of 'where the music is produced' (again, this is not a conventionally common compositional choice, but it's not difficult to imagine), it may have more impact on the sound of the music because of the resulting reverb than if they were to specify that it should be performed in a living room. Or, less tangibly, this could simply give performances a non-sonic sense of significance and ceremony. But both these effects would be simultaneous and not easily extricable as part of the whole musical experience.[7]

Non-sonic variables have a huge and often unrecognised importance for the production and experience of music. How performers look, whether they perform at night or in the day, what sort of dance the musicians and audience might be expected to perform – these may not conventionally be thought of as part of 'the music' or 'the musical work', but they are a part of *music*. Even when music comes in the form of a recording, meaning that the composers have effectively surrendered control over most of the non-sonic variables to the listener, we can think of an attribute like the decoration on the recording's case being determined by variables just as the sonic component is. The choices made through these variables can and usually does affect, often dramatically, our experience of the music just as the choices made over the sounds alone do. Clearly *there is music beyond sound*.

That non-sonic elements don't seem to be 'part of *the* music' is simply a result of the conventions that surround the way we think about what music actually is, especially in the West. These conventions suggest to us that 'a musical work *x*' exists in some abstract, virtual, immortal form that remains the same, no matter what the non-sonic circumstances of its performance might be. Performances of the work could take place at different concerts or through speakers or headphones on different occasions, it doesn't matter. In its final sense, the word *performance* here refers to any instance of music being played or in any way *actualised*, whether live or not. Each time 'a musical work *x*' is played in different circumstances, sonic or non-sonic, some attributes of the music (i.e. the values of the musical variables, making up musical information) *are* undeniably changing in actuality from performance to performance, and in ways that we may consider important. I've already suggested that electronic music can be more specific in its control over musical variables and their values than classical music usually is, and this is the same principle. Each time a single work of classical music is performed, its sonic details – some part of the musical information – change with the performer at the point of performance, such as its precise tuning, its vibrato, as well as small changes to the speeds and rhythms each time. We conventionally tend to discount these changes as not being 'part of the work', because they weren't *specified* by the composers, but are left to others or to chance.

In contrast to the way we usually talk about musical works, we could say that when we hear 'the same' work performed in two different sets of circumstances, we are in a different sense – that is, at a more advanced *degree of specification* – hearing what we could think of as two *different* musical works in actuality. We could adapt the famous saying of the Ancient Greek philosopher Heraclitus, 'one cannot step twice into the same river', and say similarly that one can't experience exactly the same musical work twice. Just as different quantities of water molecules will be in the river each time we step into it, all at different positions and momentums, the values of some variables (practically insignificant, perhaps) in the music will be different every time the work is performed. Had the composers in fact chosen to specify the values given by variables controlling precise tuning, *vibrato*, precise speed and precise volume in those two separate ways, or had the performer ignored those specifications, conventional thinking might be more likely to accept that the works were different.[8] But it must be admitted that the *music* varied and was different in ways that could have mattered a great deal to electronic composers, who may choose to have specified precision tunings, rhythms and volumes in their music.

Just as with sounds, the borders that we conventionally draw around 'pieces of music' – what is in the music and what is outside of it – are arbitrary with regard to the multitude of variations that may occur between differently specified musical actualities, and only limit our awareness of the detailed possibilities of compositional specification open to composers.[9] We could invent a kind of music that we *do* consider to be dependent on and defined by its performance in specified locations, for example, just as more traditional music is predicated upon a specified structure of pitches. Needless to say, the appreciation of such a music would be a new and unusual experience.[10] Many composers simply don't realise just how many and what types of variable they can specify in their compositions, and specify in highly complex ways, and the strange new musical practices that can result.

The same principle applies to non-sonic variables. The circumstantial changes that inevitably occur from performance to performance might indeed have consequences to the sound, such as whether the music was played in a cathedral that resulted in lots of reverb. Or they may not, as in the cases when performers of eighteenth-century classical music choose to wear eighteenth-century dress during a concert. It would be a shame and a limitation to say that the reverb, and even those costumes, should be discounted as having nothing to do with 'the music' because it does have a great effect on the concert as a unified artistic event, as an indivisible experience.

The convention that suggests that music is nothing but sound(s), or that the sound is the only relevant factor in music, could be described as *sonocentric*. It's sonocentric, for example, to believe that the best way to appreciate music is to listen intently and autonomously to 'the sounds themselves', and to regard any music that doesn't reward this mode of listening, or that incorporates a deliberate non-sonic element, as being accordingly inferior. This philosophy was highly influential in the twentieth century, and cannot reflect the true breadth of possible musical experience.

A Definition of Music

Here we've started to challenge the most basic conventional definitions of what music is. The difficulty is that if music can have non-sonic elements, then where does a concept of 'music' properly begin and end? What distinguishes musical activity from 'non-musical' activity? Is, say, the variable number of people gathered outside the concert hall during a musical performance 'part of the music', a musical variable? The answer is simple: only if it has been specified by the composers of the music playing within the concert hall or perceived and appreciated as part of the music by the listeners. In other contexts where the figure of an individual or multiple 'composer' doesn't apply, it would have to be specified in a wider cultural context of appreciation, and Western culture doesn't conventionally hold anything outside a concert hall to be musically specified. What if the composers had arranged people to gather outside another building where there weren't specified sounds going on inside? Then there would be little to distinguish those composers from that broader category of which they're a part: *artists*. What specific sorts of artists are composers then? *Composers are artists whose artistic decisions relate primarily to the production of sound.* And what (specific sort of art) is music? *Art that relates primarily to the production of sound.*

Although it makes a roughly practical amount of sense, this word 'primarily' doesn't make the definition very clear cut. But firstly, as with art itself, these distinctions aren't very clear cut, especially throughout the history and geography of the world. 'Music' is only a word, after all, and indeed, not one whose definition has an equivalent in every language. In many non-Western cultures, what we would call music is simply an aspect of the general activities of life and not a differentiable concept of its own. Besides which, many cultures don't have 'composers' in the same way that the West does, and yet they do have individuals and groups who produce music.

Secondly, is there any real need for such a clear-cut definition of music? Why shouldn't art and music overlap sometimes? Does there need to be a real, absolute, immortal distinction between the two areas? Of course not. At a further level, many artists have even thrived on the fact that the border between art and 'real life' itself is fluid, if truly there at all. This could be what the twentieth-century composer and theorist John Cage, one of the first to plumb the depths of the infinite possibilities of music, meant by the phrase he was so fond of repeating: 'everything we do is music'.

We can say that music is not a museum of unchanging sonic artifacts; instead it's an *event*, one that in actuality occurs once only. Scores, instructions and recordings specify the details of this event to a greater or lesser degree, but they don't wholly determine it, much less do they represent some 'essence' of the music. The musicologist Christopher Small was so convinced that music should be thought of as an activity that manifested in events rather than a collection of (and an opportunity to make) fixed art objects that he declared that there was no such thing as music, reinventing the concept as a verb: 'musicking'. This is how he defined it: 'to music is to take part, in any capacity, in a musical performance, whether by performing, by listening, by rehearsing or practicing, by providing material for performance (what is called composing), or by dancing.'[11] Examining the activity of musicking around the world, Small saw that what is known as music is part of a socialising and deeply ideological *ritual*, a multimedia performance art that cannot be reduced to sound or score. This was even true in the Western classical tradition, where a contrasting ideology of art-for-art's-sake sonic autonomy is routinely assumed. Non-sonic variables can't ultimately be discarded, say, as music's incidental 'packaging' because they are an important part of the ritual itself and are inextricable from it; there never was any absolute difference between packaging and what was inside.

In order to appreciate the full range of possible musical specifications in a composition, we shouldn't think of 'a piece of music' in the conventional sense – as a fixed and passively experienced sound object – but rather of musical events, such as concerts or the playing of personal mp3 players (which amount to the same thing), over which composers have varying degrees of specific control. Listening and participating in any way, too, makes you a part of that event. Music is not just something you listen to, it's something that happens, something you're involved in – something you do.

Constraining Variables: Quantisation

So far we've gathered a truly vast number of potential musical choices for composers. Many different variables can describe the qualitative and quantitative attributes of music, and can be applied at any and every level, scale or point within music-making, from the miniscule details of short sounds, to sections of musical works, to whole collections of performances. Some variables can be thought of as having the activity of other variables implicated 'within' them, such as texture or whether reverb is switched on or off at a point within the music. Some variables describe the interrelationships between parts of the music and other variables. There are even non-sonic variables, describing aspects of the music that lie beyond the merely sonic, which could be taken into account as part of music. Now let's multiply those possibilities even further by looking at the ways in which the values given by variables can be measured and constrained within musical composition. How the values expressed by a variable are measured or constrained, and thus how its variability is expressed in music, is itself yet another variable that composers can take into account and manipulate, of course.

Let's take a common – almost too common – musical variable: pitch. How is it measured? In the context of conventional Western classical music it's measured in the notes of the equally tempered scale. There are twelve of these notes in an octave, each equally spaced apart by the interval of a semitone. This isn't the only way to measure pitch, however. There are other ways to divide up the octave too, resulting in alternative scales. Many musical cultures divide octaves into five or sometimes seven unevenly spaced notes. The twentieth-century composer Harry Partch invented a scale that divided the octave into forty-three notes. In all these cases, the variable of pitch is measured using division of the octave into a series of separate or *discrete* steps.

Pitch values don't have to be thought of as a series of discrete steps, however. Scientists, engineers and many composers measure pitch in terms of the frequency at which a sound wave oscillates, given by the standard unit of measurement for frequency, the hertz, which represents the number of oscillations or 'cycles' per second. Theoretically, pitch can be measured to an extremely specific or infinitesimal accuracy in hertz by using a correspondingly long or infinite number of decimal places. Because with hertz frequency isn't measured in terms of discrete steps but can be specified to a theoretically infinite degree, using them recognises that the values given by the variable of pitch can be *continuous* – they form an unbroken line, in contrast to the steps formed by discrete scale notes. With hertz, pitches are *continuous with each other*.

When composers impose a scale onto the variable of pitch, so that the values of that variable are divided up, measured in or converted into discrete steps rather than treated continuously, we say they are *quantising* the variable of pitch. To *quantise* a variable is to constrain its continuous values into a prescribed series or set of discrete steps or units, thus ignoring, preventing or imperfectly approximating whatever values may lie 'in between' those steps. Quantisation turns a *continuous variable* into a *discrete variable*. We could call the reverse *dequantisation*. Choosing how variables may be quantised is very important in musical composition. It's usually an unappreciated compositional choice, as prior, readymade quantisations are routinely an unquestioned aspect of musical technology, especially with many more traditional instruments.

When continuous values are quantised, they are in effect 'rounded up' or 'rounded down' to the nearest discrete step. Sometimes this discrete step can simply be a whole number – a musical variable 'number of people clapping their hands' can't have continuous values because people are measured in whole numbers, and they're either clapping or they aren't. Similarly, binary variables can be thought of as already quantised, as in the case of the reverb being either on or off – there are no in-between values. Again, the values of variables are like their 'settings', with the reverb in this case having just 'on' and 'off' settings. If we wanted more precise control over the reverb, a different variable could describe some aspect of its magnitude, such as the volume of the processed sound relative to that of the original sound, which is known as the 'wetness' of the reverb. This variable could have continuous values, expressed as a percentage with a theoretically infinite number of decimal places.

Time, too, is measured and quantised in some way in most musical performances. An underlying, generally even pulse divides up time like the markings on a ruler in most Western music, and the pulse's speed is described using words (such as, traditionally, the Italian *adagio*, 'leisurely', or *allegro*, 'brisk') or expressed as a number of beats per minute. In some musics this pulse or the subdivisions of it are less even. The durations of modern Western classical notation are quantised as regular subdivisions (using the British vocabulary): a breve consists of two semibreves, which consists of two minims, which consists of two crotchets, which consists of two quavers or eight semiquavers or sixteen demisemiquavers and so on, all of which can be divided into 'tuplets' of three, five, seven and so on. These discrete values are then, at one level or another, fitted to the underlying pulse. Durations are then added together using ties, or increased by one and a half their length by marking a dot after the note.

Theoretically, this quantisation system allows for continuous values of time position and duration because notes can be divided into two *ad infinitum*, but in practice composers rarely move beyond the level of the demisemiquaver. Needless to say, this system has largely discouraged the specific notation of more subtle and irregular rhythms, particularly because they're awkward to read and write on the page, not to mention perform. In fact, as with vibrato, Western classical performers regularly warp the underlying pulse themselves in order to express emotion, speeding up and slowing down in a technique called *rubato* (*tempo rubato* means 'stolen time') in ways that would be very difficult for classical composers to notate traditionally. Again, electronic composers can specify the values of rubato variables themselves, though the subtle rhythms they can construct needn't have anything to do with traditional rubato method. They could warp the pulse across longer or shorter amounts of time than classical rubato does, for example, 'stealing' any amount of time they liked, wherever they liked.

Time, of course, can be expressed as a continuous value, measured in milliseconds, seconds, minutes, hours, days etc. Many electronic composers control time variables this way, and the values they choose are only quantised by the capability of their equipment to accurately express miniscule lengths of time (computers, for example, have a finite number of binary code digits or 'bits' through which sounds can be expressed). Or within a process of composition (electronic or not), we may wish to quantise the durations of notes to, say, seconds or half seconds, just for the sake of interest or a certain coherent consistency.

The size of each step created in quantising a variable doesn't have to correspond to the same amount in the original continuous values. When quantising pitch using the Western classical equal temperament system, for example, the step represented by each scale note doesn't equal the same amount of hertz. I didn't define the octave before: a sound's pitch is increased by the interval of an octave when its frequency is doubled. The pitch called 'A4', the first A above 'Middle C' (which is roughly at the centre of a conventional piano's keyboard), is fixed at approximately 440Hz, though it varies in practice. The next octave up, that is the next A, is approximately 880Hz, the next is 1760Hz and so on. So the step through an amount of hertz represented by a scale note actually gets larger and larger each time as successively higher adjacent notes are played. This nonetheless sounds evenly spaced due to the construction of the human ear, but there are any number of ways – or formulas – in which the values given by musical variables can be 'unevenly' quantised in similar ways. To stretch the technical definition of the term slightly, quantisation could even be an arbitrary or random process where steps are uneven and don't follow any formula. Playing a randomly tuned piano could be an interesting way of exploring and expressing the variable of pitch, for example.

For many variables, quantisation is relatively simple. Where a variable can't easily be reduced to a single scale of continuous measurement, this is because the activity of other variables is already implicated within it. This was the case with the variable of texture, which can be broken down into interrelating pitch, time position and duration variables. Because texture is a relation of variable pitches, durations and positions in time, it can't be reduced to hertz or seconds and then quantised to scale notes or, say, crotchets. Though I named it as an example of a basic musical variable (and it is), timbre also presents this problem. There is no unit of measurement for timbre, no single line along which continuous values can be specified. Pitch values are somewhere between high and low, time values are somewhere between long and short, volume values are somewhere between loud and soft, but timbre can be, a lot more vaguely, 'harsh' or 'smooth', 'full-bodied' or 'thin', 'muffled' or 'clear' and more besides. This is because timbre, like texture, already has the activity of many variables implicated within it, even if it might not seem like it at first, and as such can be 'broken down' into more fundamental variables. Unlike texture, however, the variables implicated within the category called timbre are not always the same, or so simple.

Many factors can go into determining the attributes of timbre. In acoustic music these are the dimensions and materials of the instruments, which control how the original vibration is produced and how the sound echoes, resonates or is absorbed as it's played. In a synthesiser, the waveform of the sound-making oscillation can be given by electrically representing mathematical functions (such as a sine wave) or choosing from a selection of presets. All result in different timbres, but after this frequencies can be filtered and resonance added to sculpt the timbre further. In fact, however they're produced or whatever pitch they're at, most timbres can be thought of as a combination of a number of 'voices' (sometimes called 'overtones') that have different waveforms, frequencies, volumes and time positions within their oscillation all added together to make a single waveform. Timbre depends on frequency, volume and time, and can usually be broken down into those variables.[12] Using computers, composers can effectively create their own new timbres by manipulating those variables at small scales.

Timbre may not be amenable to a single form of measurement in the same way that pitch is, but can it be quantised? For many composers working before the invention of the synthesiser, it effectively was – *as a choice between a selection of separate instruments.* Just as for most composers control over pitch was restricted to the twelve notes of the scale, so their control over timbre was restricted to whatever instruments were available and the limited ways in which performers could modify their timbres (by using mutes, etc.). This is to expand the idea of quantisation a little beyond its strict definition, where it tends to pertain to a single set of values, but in practice instruments are *discrete* in the same way that scale notes are. Unless they were willing to invent their own instruments and thus step outside the conventional system, timbre was not a freely continuous variable as it can be with modern technology, but one confined to the discrete 'presets' that are instruments. We can expand the definition of quantisation, then: *to quantise a variable is to restrict its possible values to a number of apparently discrete options.* In effect, quantisation turns a choice of 'what' into a choice of 'which'.

Constraining Variables: Limiting Ranges

The process of quantisation constrains how composers can make choices within the locus of a single variable. Let's now look at constraints on variables in a slightly more general sense. I've already discussed a number of times how the values given by variables can be specified to different extents and in different contexts, and it's worth focusing on this before we go any further.

In many contexts, the choice composers have over the values given by a variable is, or can be, limited to a certain *range*. Again, the size and position of the range imposed on a variable can be given as values of further variables, those dictating the range's size. Musical instruments all have certain limited ranges of pitches they can play, for example, whether the variable of pitch is quantised or not. Loudspeakers have a maximum and minimum volume. Effects in electronic music have certain upper and lower limits on the values of the variables they control. Instruments have timbral limits – for example, a violin can't produce the timbre of a trumpet. Instruments also have textural limits – a single oboe can only play one scale note at a time (i.e. it's limited to a monophonic texture), and a single six-stringed guitar can't play more than six at a time (this usually means, but isn't limited to, six scale notes in quick succession, according to the conventional playing technique of strumming). Musical instruments are contexts in which musical variability is quantised and limited in various specific ways. (Quantisation can be thought of as a type of range limitation, since a range doesn't have to set up a single, unbroken boundary on variability. There can in effect be multiple different discrete 'ranges' applied to a set of values, equivalent to the 'steps' created by quantisation. Whereas quantisation constrains continuous values into discrete steps, a more general notion of range limitation can apply to both discrete and continuous variables.)

In musical instruments, the constraints imposed on variability are physical limitations, the result of technical matters of design. Very often, though, such constraints are the result of conventional practice within a certain physical or stylistic context. Take the variable of duration, for example. Other than in the context of limited personal or physical energy resources and the eventual destruction of the Earth or the universe, there's no upper limit on the duration of a sound. Within the context of Western classical conventions, however (which we needn't define precisely, only statistically), durations of notes rarely exceed a length of twenty seconds. John Cage composed a piece for organ instructively entitled $Organ^2/ASLSP$ *(As SLow aS Possible)* – with the help of an air-blowing machine and a suitable method of keeping the keys pressed, a well-maintained conventional pipe organ can hold a note indefinitely. A performance of $Organ^2/ASLSP$ started at an abandoned church in Halberstadt, Germany in 2001 and is scheduled to finish in the year 2639. Even this length of time could be construed as a conservative estimation of what is 'possible' when it comes to duration – Cage's piece demands the very limits of physical possibility.[13] At the other end of the scale, discrete sounds are rarely shorter than around ten milliseconds in conventional Western classical music.

To specify a certain value for a variable at any point whatsoever in music is to impose a limitation on the possible range of that variable's variability within a certain context. If the range is zero, then the note is precisely defined. Composers may specify that a sound will have a pitch of precisely 440Hz, with an implied range of zero around that one point on the continuous pitch line. Or those composers may specify that a pitch be between 420Hz and 460Hz, giving a range of 40Hz, so that it can vary between actual performances. This is in effect what happens when Western classical composers write the note A4 in a score – when it's played by a performer, that note may have any pitch within approximately that range (the range isn't precisely defined). We see once again how electronic composers can be more precise in the values given by variables than Western classical composers.

This potential to give precise values for variables is appealing, as it can bring a whole host of subtleties into music that were previously unknown and that composers are only just beginning to discover and use effectively. But I must emphasise that this closer precision at the level of performance is not necessarily any more preferable than allowing values to vary between performances within certain ranges. Remember, our purpose is to discover the maximum possibilities of music, to maximise music to the utmost degree. That includes music with built-in flexibility as well as music that's richly precise in its details. Composers may choose to specify that a certain sound be within a range of 151Hz to 897Hz, they may then choose to quantise that length in some way so that the performer then has a number of options within that range. Such a specification rarely happens, since the instructions given to performers of improvised music conventionally tend to be less specific than this – but thinking about range limitation on variables allows us to imagine music with such levels of specification.

Flexible Music and Concrete Music
Music like this, in which any kind of range of variability is effectively permitted at the point of performance, could be called *flexible music*. Flexible music leaves the actual, infinitely specific values chosen for each individual performance to chance or to the choice of the performers. We could also call it *music with moving parts*: like any object with points of movement and ranges imposed on that movement, flexible music can occupy a range of different states in different performances or at certain points in time within those performances.[14] An object like a plastic doll similarly has moving parts – it may be able to rotate both its arms independently at the shoulders so that each may occupy any

point within a circle, say, but may not be able to move its head or vary any other part. The doll would then have two points of movement, two variables that could differ within certain ranges (we can call these *degrees of freedom*), giving it the ability to be 'posed' in different ways. An artist's dummy has many more points of movement, and with wider ranges of movements, so it can offer a far greater selection of poses. Flexible music, music with moving parts, can be 'posed' in different ways like this – *the 'same' music can manifest in different ways at the point of actual performance*. We could say that flexible music can be *actualised* in different ways at the point of performance. In a single performance we experience just one snapshot, one actualisation of the music's potential variability, just as if we were to present an artist's dummy frozen in one particular pose.

Flexible music is a music-making context that leaves the precise values of at least one variable with some room for its values to differ within a range. As we've seen, the performance of traditional Western classical music at a concert is flexible – the precise values for pitch are quantised to scale notes, but the range of pitch allowed around those scale notes is relatively flexible. Generally if a player is more than half a semitone out of tune, that's considered a problem. Volumes, too, are relatively flexible in Western classical music, both individually and relative to one another. Composers mark *forte* or *f* for loud volumes and *piano* or *p* for soft volumes and other markings are derived from these, but these don't correspond to precise measurements of volume in decibels (as they might do in electronic music, for example), so they do vary between actual performances.

In Western classical music from the nineteenth century onwards, the notes specified by composers had to be played more or less exactly by the performer (before that, performers were often allowed to 'decorate' notes and melodies with trills and turns or improvise during the cadenza section of a concerto), but musical traditions such as jazz are somewhat more flexible in this area. In much live jazz music, there are sections where performers may choose their own notes and rhythms, improvising in line with underlying harmonies using certain harmonic rules which themselves became more flexible over time, until the 'free jazz' of the nineteen-fifties and sixties, which effectively disregarded any and all harmonic or scalic convention.

Around this time many composers branched off from the Western classical tradition to create musical works that allowed for a range of widely different outcomes in performance. This music often presents the performer with a set of instructions for music-making – sometimes these instructions shape the outcome of the music by incorporating improvisation, aleatory processes (which produce random outcomes, for example flipping coins or rolling dice) or deterministic processes (*algorithms*: sets of specific instructions for reaching a conclusion in a finite series of steps, or *heuristics*: more general problem-solving strategies), or some combination of these methods. John Cage was the most famous of the these composers – note that the instruction 'as long as possible' in his *Organ²/ASLSP* will give rise to different precise values of duration in actual performance – whose work was often termed 'experimental' (less technically, of course, the word 'experimental' also tends to refer to music that is unusual or ground-breaking in a more general sense). Though its duration was precisely given, Cage's most notorious work 4′ 33″ has no direct sound-making instructions in it at all. It's regularly described as a 'silent piece', but in fact it was intended as four minutes and thirty-three seconds in which any unplanned sonic event in the ambience of the performing environment could take place. More like four minutes and thirty-three seconds of general, uninterrupted listening to the world, it wouldn't have been ruined by the sound of the audience shifting in their seats or the distant noises of vehicles or creatures, and as such it's an example of a highly flexible music. Other experimental composers present performers with 'graphic scores' – pictures that may or may not incorporate traditional notation symbols, with the usual instruction being that the performers make some effort to translate that particular picture into music with varying degrees of regulation.

Conversely, we can call music that isn't flexible *concrete music*.[15] As its name suggests, concrete music is 'set in stone'. It will not change in the slightest detail from performance to performance, at least not intentionally. Essentially, concrete music is music that exists solely in the form of a recording, although there can be music that incorporates recorded or concrete elements and still differs at the point of performance and is thus flexible. Live performers don't necessarily have to have been recorded in concrete music – the sound in all its precise detail could have originated in a machine and subsequently gone straight to the recording medium (vinyl, tape, CD, mp3), a practice that's become increasingly commonplace in recent decades. Concrete composers can record live into the recording medium or computer and then manipulate those sounds using electrical equipment, or they could take samples from other recordings, cutting, editing and looping them, as in styles like hip hop. Modern pop singles rely on the editing and sound engineering of a studio, so in that form they're an example of concrete music, even if the 'same' song is also performed with minor variations as flexible music live at concerts.

As I explained earlier, some value in the music always inevitably vary from performance to performance, even beyond the level of recording. Music is different every time; we can't experience exactly the same music twice. Since what we call concrete music is no exception to this – variations in playback equipment and acoustics will cause the sonic attributes of the music to differ at the point of performance even if the effect is often practically negligible – the idea of musical concreteness can't ultimately apply, but is instead a relative term. In the end, all music is flexible if we're to consider it as having some continuing, abstracted existence beyond the single actualisation of the performance event, that single frozen 'pose'. We can only understand and believe in a 'concrete music' if we discount certain variables: we have to discount the minor effects of variable equipment and acoustics, as well as a whole host of non-sonic variables in order for a concept of concrete music, where 'the same' music can be repeated, to mean anything. Mp3 files on an mp3 player, for example, could appropriately be called concrete music despite the fact that the listeners' ability to adjust the volume of the mp3 player technically makes performances of them a clear instance of flexible music – in this case volume is the variable that's discounted in order to allow us to term the music 'concrete'.[16]

Now as we're thinking about the maximum possibilities of music here, we should be reluctant *ultimately* to discount any variables at all from composition or listening. However, it's certainly practical in the context of early twenty-first century music-making we're familiar with to differentiate between the mediums of concrete music and flexible music, as long as we don't consider this difference to be an absolute categorical distinction. Indeed, modern composers would do well to bear in mind the rich potential of both categories in themselves, and create concrete music that takes full advantage of its concreteness (its potential for precise specification), and flexible music that takes full advantage of its flexibility (its capacity to differ) – rather than finding themselves unwittingly lost in a grey zone between the two, resulting in unplanned flexibilities and relative concretenesses in the music.

But since 'concreteness' in music is relative, this dichotomy of concrete and flexible music is not a choice of 'either / or', but rather one of different relative degrees of flexibility in music-making contexts. We could say that, in a practical sense at least, music as we typically understand it exists somewhere between two poles of infinite flexibility and infinite concreteness rather than actually reaching and occupying these states.

Configurations of Musical Variables: Instruments

Let's return to the idea of flexible music, in which variables can take on any values within certain ranges. Composers may choose to specify a certain timbre and a certain quantised frequency range for music-making and then leave performers to do whatever they wanted with those values in performance, whether within the context of a specific performance event or not, thus creating a context for flexible music. If composers were to do this, they would have effectively invented what we might recognise as a *musical instrument*. This instrument might only 'exist' as a set of instructions for music-making and require other sound-making equipment to realise it, but its constrained range of variability echoes the more physical constraints imposed on musical variability that we find in conventional instruments.

Consider more conventional musical instruments similarly, as collections of constrained variables. A single piano can play a limited range of quantised pitches, a limited range of continuous volumes and effectively only a single, specific timbre. A harpsichord is the same, but the range of volumes at which it can play is a lot more limited – in some harpsichords, alternative keyboards or an array of pedals allow the performer to switch between different preset volumes and timbres, so those variables are effectively quantised. A trombone can play one timbre, a limited range of pitches, quite a wide range of volumes, and can slide through pitch as a continuous value. Turning to the variable of duration: an organ can hold a note indefinitely, the durations a trombone can play are limited by the size and strength of its performer's lungs, while the durations a xylophone can play are usually precise, unchanging, and barely endure at all. Instruments that can apply mutes, such as brass instruments, can play a limited range of timbres, and for them the variability of timbre is quantised to the array of mutes available (in the majority of cases this is a binary variable giving the values 'mute present' or 'mute absent'). Organs and other keyboards with an array of preset timbres have an accordingly more complicated range and quantisation of timbres. A synthesiser can control far more variables than pitch and volume, and many can change variables implicated within timbre continuously within wide ranges.

We notice that each instrument presents a certain *configuration* of musical variables: a collection of certain musical variables together with their assigned values. Or to put it in better detail, configurations are collections of certain musical variables together with certain quantisations and ranges imposed on them that serve to assign values to some degree of relative specificity. Again, we can think of these as a certain configuration of 'settings' on an electrical appliance or a computer program, but also bearing in mind that the values of some of these variables can be concrete or flexible. Because these configurations comprise of a limited number of variables, and because they have quantisations or ranges imposed on the values of those variables (both are 'limits'), we can refer to them as *limited configurations*. These configurations are higher structures that are 'built up' by the activity of variables just as textures and timbres are, effectively 'clustered together', with limits imposed on those variables. In such a configuration some variables are fixed to specific values (such as a piano's timbre), while others are flexible, offering a range of values (such as a piano's pitch).

Note that all of the musical instruments described above could play a range of pitches. This is certainly not always the case: a simple drum (one that can't be adjusted) can only play at one pitch, though it may be able to play at different volumes and timbres by hitting the drum with varying force and at the centre or edge of the skin. We could even imagine an instrument that could only play one very specific pitch, but had a wide range of continuous variables controlling duration, volume, timbre and other variables like reverb and distortion – such an instrument wasn't invented for Western classical music, because that tradition privileges change in the variable of pitch particularly highly. Without any modifications, an air horn like those used at a sporting event or attached to a vehicle can play one pitch at one volume with one timbre and can endure for as long as its player wants within the limited range that the air can last, so effectively only the variable of duration is left with a range of variability in this case.

Some air horns, in particular the handheld, gas-powered variety, have a specific way in which they decrease to a steady pitch over a certain length of time – also an attribute that isn't flexible. A configuration of variables whose given values change through certain points in the duration of the sound is called the *envelope* of that sound. An airhorn has one precise envelope that remains the same each time it's played. Many synthesisers can vary the envelopes of the sounds they make, usually in four phases: attack (a starting value and an attack point value, given by a variable such as volume or pitch, and the length of time taken to go from one value to the other), decay (a specific value and the length of time taken to reach that value after the attack point passes), sustain (a specific value that will pertain indefinitely as long as the note is held) and release (a specific value and the length of time taken to reach that value once the note is released – conventionally, sounds decay away to nothing or zero at this point much like reverb, but they could, for example, increase in pitch during the decay period and then suddenly stop.)

Acoustic instruments have envelopes too – a piano has a long decay period and a sustain point of zero volume because the sound dies away to nothing even while a key is held down. Pianos have practically no attack period, and when the sustaining pedal is held down, the notes acquire a long release period and much longer decay periods than otherwise. Pipe organs don't have attack, decay or release periods (unless we take into account the reverb of the building it's in – sometimes it's a reverb-causing stone church – as a release period, though the same applies to any instrument), but they do sustain, unlike a piano. Unlike many synthesiser settings, most acoustic instruments don't have very exaggerated or even noticeable envelopes.

Configurations of Musical Variables: Styles

The constraints imposed on variability by limited configurations can be less obvious than those of a musical instrument's physical properties, however, and can operate at every different level of music-making. A range or a quantisation can be imposed on a variable at the level of a subsection of a musical work, an entire musical work, an instrument, a style, an entire musical tradition or at any point beyond or in between these conceptual layers. Accordingly, limited configurations of variables can operate at any level of music-making, and imagining music as consisting of them can give us a clear view of what variable structures make up musical activity and how they relate.

One thing we realise when thinking of music in terms of limited configurations of variables is that a musical instrument and a musical style (e.g. dub reggae, doom metal, bebop jazz, eighteenth-century Viennese classical, minimal techno, Indian Carnatic music, etc.) are not so different in kind. Both are particular sets of rules that guide and constrain the formal potential of music-making, and as such, both are configurations of variables in which some values are fixed while others may vary. Both are templates or guidelines for which variables' values can change in music: which values can change, which values stay the same, and how.

Now of course, the ranges and constraints imposed on instruments are physical while those imposed on styles, though perhaps partly physical, are to some extent culturally conventional. Composers can stretch and modify the rules of musical styles as they wish – in doing this they may not always be understood by those who appreciate the style under its previous terms, but they usually can do this to some degree. Because of this, the constraints imposed on variables in particular styles are not absolute, but can only be given as a statistically derived impression, as a structure emerging from averages and regularly recurring patterns in the activity of variables, observed in a sample population of recordings or performances up to the present time.

Besides, as limited musical configurations, styles are usually a lot more complex than instruments, with more variables coming into play and interacting in more intricate ways. Styles can present a very particular set of rules that are always observed, or they can be very loose and divergent. They can be talked about at many different levels or sizes too – a single composer or group of composers or a work with many movements (such as a symphony or the modern album) can have its own uniquely identifiable style, but so can a culture, a country or a period in time. Styles can give a specific form to music-making in the context of small communities at very particular times (say a matter of weeks) all the way up to the rich and enormously varying traditions of entire continents over centuries, of which Western classical music, if we choose to talk about it as a whole, is an example.

In many styles, the values that remain fixed from performance to performance are those of speed, texture, volume and formal structure across time. Thrash metal music is usually relatively fast, while Japanese Gagaku music is usually relatively slow (at least regarding its distribution of sonic events). Unaccompanied barbershop quartet singing usually has a very tight, generally homophonic texture, while many composers of twentieth-century classical music were known for creating sparse and disconnected textures. Most rock music is loud, while ambient music tends to be quiet. The structures of Medieval

European songs usually stayed very specific from song to song, while trance dance music has an equally specific yet very different structural behaviour in time. In all these styles the attributes described tend to remain invariant but the pitches, durations and other variables may vary within a certain range. Likewise, in some styles the timbres vary within a range, in some they remain the same. Acid house dance music of the late eighties was perhaps the first identified electronic style to be heavily characterised by a very specific timbre that remained the same from track to track. Sometimes described as a 'squelch' sound, it had a distinctive envelope and was created using certain settings on the Roland TB-303 Bass Line synthesiser. Similarly, the jungle dance music that followed some years later tended to draw on a very limited range of pre-existing samples for its percussion.

In many styles, harmonic practices are constrained and regulated: early blues music is often very specific in this regard, with much of it following the 'twelve bar blues' template. Mode – the word essentially refers to the type of scale, 'major' and 'minor' are modes – is usually fixed, or fixed within a certain limited structure governing its change. Or specific intervals and even melodic fragments tend to be preferred: in many areas of contemporary classical music, intervals and groups of intervals are routinely arranged so as to avoid the conventions of what is called 'common practice tonality', with the result that it sounds dissonant to many people. In early twenty-first-century grime music, from London, minor seconds and thirds (intervals of a semitone or three semitones respectively) are often favoured in the riddims (the instrumental backing to the MCs) as they can harmonically create a feeling of danger.

Thinking of styles as templates for how values change or remain the same reveals some of the biases in variability that stylistic conventions set up. For example, you rarely see musical styles in which the specific pitches remain the same but other variables vary, or at least we don't conventionally call these musical styles, but there's no reason why they shouldn't exist. One example could be Gregorian or other monastic chant dating back to the Early Medieval period, where the specific rows of pitches written in the liturgy are used again and again over the centuries. What little we know about the practices of liturgical singing in the Medieval period would seem to suggest that while the rows of notes remained more or less the same, the volumes, speeds, durations, decorations and even rhythms probably varied widely from monastery to monastery throughout Europe.

Configurations of Musical Variables: Works

Both musical instruments and musical styles are examples of flexible music. They're not individual flexible musical works, but they're no less flexible: as limited configurations they can give rise to different musical outcomes in performance. This means that a musical instrument or a musical style and a flexible musical work are, in just the same way, not so different in kind either. Again, instruments, styles and musical works are all alike in being limited configurations of variables where some values are more fixed than others.

Aside from cultural convention, one of the things that does set these three categories apart, of course, is their relationship to time. By themselves, instruments don't exist within a finite time continuum of music-making, unlike most musical works. Each note an instrument plays may be controlled over time by an envelope, but unlike most musical works an instrument doesn't set up a single length of time in which all those notes exist. We can also talk about instruments as they exist within the context of musical works (the bass guitar in a particular song, for example), but the fact remains: instruments themselves are music-making devices, actualising music but constrained in variability, just as much as a symphony or a song or a melody is. Put simply, *a musical instrument is a musical work without a time limit*. It operates outside of and between the time-limited performances of musical works in their traditional sense.

Style is the same. We could say the late Romantic symphonic style usually gives rise to musical works that exceed twenty minutes, and thus styles can feature specified total durations. But again, a single musical work sets up a finite time continuum in which all its variability takes place, while a style will give rise to many different time continuums and exists as a statistical entity outside of and between each of those individual continuums (that is, performance events). There is no ultimately necessary distinction between the two categories, because all time continuums, whether music happens within them or outside of and between them, *are no more or less the domain of musical variables than any other structure within music.* Durations can apply in many ways to music-making, none of them essential. They can be 'nested' into one another, creating constrained durations within constrained durations. For example, a note can have an envelope lasting half a second and be just a part of a sample lasting three seconds, which goes into forming a phrase lasting six seconds, which goes into forming a section lasting thirty seconds in a piece lasting two minutes (and any one of these lengths could have more flexible values, incidentally). Music can be flexible outside of any single time continuum given for its actualisation, and instruments and styles are among the examples of this sort of musical structure.

Thinking of instruments and styles as configurations of variables just like musical works, which makes them all level within the same category, suggests to us that instruments and styles deserve status as musical 'art objects' just as much as musical works do. Like musical works, they create musical performances, and so what if those performances happen to be flexible, differing more than those of conventional musical works? Experimental musical works can differ at the point of performance too, and often just as much. We conventionally think of instruments and styles as subordinate or incidental to the category of musical works, but they are the 'art objects' that make up music as a whole no less than musical works are.

Configurations and the Variability of Music as a Whole

So whatever sort of time continuums they do or don't occupy, everything we may wish to talk about in music-making, any entity or structure within music, is a limited configuration, a cluster of musical variables where some may be more flexible than others and some may have ranges imposed on them. A homophonic, monophonic or any other texture is a configuration of variables: remember how we can break texture down into the 'smaller' variables of pitch and time – this is because it's a specific configuration of those variables. In just the same way, a melody is a configuration of variables, a drum loop, a chord, a collection of chords, a reverb effect, a certain timbre, the ending of a certain musical work, an ensemble of performers, a set of speakers – all can be thought of as limited configurations of musical variables. Music as a whole is a vast rolling sea of variables, all potentially equal in importance, with changing values – sometimes still, sometimes gently shifting, sometimes surging heavily – and all grouping together in any and every way to create an astonishing variety of different forms and practices of varying flexibilities, many of which we have yet to imagine, let alone define and use.

Musical styles, musical works and musical instruments are all alike in being specific manifestations of music's infinite potential for variability. As such, we could even say that they're the same type of entity and simply assigned to different classes by the conventions of language, owing to the presence or absence of certain variables and their activity (such as those of time continuums and whether they're inside or outside of them). Add or subtract some variables, or adjust some values and constraints even by just a tiny, virtually infinitesimal amount, and we can transform any configuration of musical variables into another possible configuration, a process that can be repeated endlessly to generate an infinite number of configurations. Because of the ability to move seamlessly between possible configurations this way, we can begin to see that styles, works, instruments and all possible configurations of musical variables are ultimately *continuous with each other*, and that the terms we use to separate these specific types of music and music-making are simply the result of the way we effectively *quantise musical activity with the language and concepts we use*. Remember, musical variables that are built up from multiple 'smaller' variables into more complex structures can be quantised too, just as timbre was quantised to a selection of instruments and texture is quantised into concepts of 'homophonic', 'monophonic' and so on. As such, every musical structure, no matter how complex, is a quantisation – a making discrete – of music's continuous variability.

This is why it doesn't initially seem to make sense to talk about a musical instrument that can vary hugely in timbre but not in pitch,[17] or a style of music where the series of pitches is the same in each performance but the rhythms vary.[18] Seeing music only through such seemingly discrete concepts as 'style', 'work', 'instrument', 'melody', 'rhythm', 'notes' and indeed 'sounds' makes it difficult for us to imagine the configurations of variables *outside of* and *between* these categories for which there are no existing terms or concepts (yet) – configurations that might appear to be, say, part style, part instrument, or part melody, part timbre, or part texture, part timbre and part rhythm. Even describing these configurations as combinations of pre-existing concepts is crude and insufficient regarding the breadth of forms that configurations of musical variables can take. It's difficult to describe configurations that don't fall neatly into the categories of 'works', 'instruments' or 'styles' using existing concepts from language, but we should try. All these concepts hide from us the pure, complete potential for variability in music, its utmost possibilities and combinations, its continuous, pre-quantised, pre-constrained infinity.

This is why it's so important and so inspiring to think of music in terms of the variables from which it's created, as a *complex system of variables relating to the production of sound.* Music's variable attributes come before the rules, discrete concepts and labels we impose on it, and will remain even if all those rules and concepts melt away. No one musical variable or collection of musical variables, or quantisation or range limitation (these are variables too), is necessary for the creation of music, but all are sufficient, and all can be applied in any way or in any combination at all.

Musical variables are the paths that the imaginations of composers and listeners may tread – each is a certain locus of possibilities. Some paths are more beaten than others. Imagine a discrete concept or sound by itself, and it's only so easy to imagine it being any different. Imagine a variable of pitch, and you can imagine a virtually infinite number of pitches from very low to very high values. Better still, imagine a discrete concept or sound as something created by a configuration of musical variables, and you can imagine adding or removing variables, changing values and the flexibility of those values – you have easy access to a whole host of new forms that differ in new and strange ways from the all-too-familiar sounds and concepts that lie behind us. We can begin to see how, especially with the help of modern music technology, composers may control the activity of variables with precision and at any and every level of specification (far beyond the physical and mental capabilities of traditional human performers), and even outside of the conventional boundaries and modes of music-making, which dissolve as a result.

If composers are truly to take advantage of music's utmost possibilities and set out into that vast sea of musical variability along a new route, they must *dequantise* what they know – break it down into its rawer, continuous variability – and then *requantise* by creating strange new configurations of musical variables from what they find. These new configurations may be re-used and explored in detail, but they, too, may ultimately be dequantised. Composers can keep themselves and their listeners constantly mindful of music's full potential for variability by continually *dequantising, requantising, and dequantising again,* and by finding some equilibrium between the rule-breaking of dequantisation and the rule-making of quantisation.

In the next part we'll give that sea of musical variability a name – *music space* – and we'll see how the configurations that make it up (or what I'll call *musical objects*) can be described in more detail. We'll describe them as 'spaces' of possibility set up by variables and values, and we'll look at how these music spaces can give rise to increasingly specific and complex information.

Part 2: Welcome to Music Space

We've seen that music – and everything that includes – can be thought of as a complex system of musical variables relating to the production of sound. Musical variables don't just describe the attributes of, circumstances of and interrelationships within that sound – their activity, that is, the ever-changing values they express, effectively creates music. We've considered that rather than amounting to a collection of static art objects, music is actualised in performance events, and that musical variables can detail the attributes of those events to relative degrees of specification. Musical variables can be sonic or non-sonic, and the values they give can be flexible (that is, they have certain freedoms to differ at the point of performance, perhaps within a limited range or quantisation) or concrete (that is, they are precisely specified by composers, not taking into account any other variability between performances). Musical variables and the values they give can be grouped together to form configurations that can accordingly be flexible or concrete, and it is these configurations – whether they set up a single time continuum of performance to exist within (as most musical works do) or not (as is the case with instruments or styles, concepts which apply outside of the individual time continuums of performances or works) – that make up music.

The instruments, styles, musical works and concepts we know and may have identifying names for are all limited configurations of musical variables in this way, but there are countless other possible configurations 'between them', yet to be discovered and used. Any adjustment of musical variables or their values can turn one possible configuration into another possible configuration, so all of these configurations can ultimately be seen to be continuous with each other. Each configuration is only one particular, specific form that will always be a limitation of and within music's continuous variability as a whole. For these reasons, composers and listeners should try to remain mindful of music's pure, unlimited, unspecified and unquantised potential to vary, even though our music-making activities are necessarily constrained to such particular forms.

In this part, we'll refer to that variability of music as a whole as *music space*. I've already described music space as a 'sea' and suggested that specific variables can be thought of as 'paths' or 'routes' through it. Calling this total variability a 'space' continues the analogy, imagining musical possibility in a similarly geometrical or geographical way. We'll also refer to limited configurations of musical variables together with the constraints (i.e. quantisations, ranges) imposed on the values of those variables as *musical objects*. This is both for the sake of convenience and because those limited configurations are the objects that make up music, where terms like 'sounds', 'melodies', 'pieces of music' and 'instruments' are, as we've seen, either too vague or too specific as concepts. Music space, then, is the *continuous space* or *continuum formed by all musical objects*.

Cage's 'Sound Space'

John Cage was one of the first theorists of composition to discuss a 'space' of maximum musical possibilities. In 1957, in a lecture about experimental music and the sonic potential of new tape recording technologies, Cage described a space through which any sound could be created:

> The situation made available by [tape recording and manipulation technology] is essentially a total sound space, the limits of which are ear-determined only, the position of a particular sound in this space being the result of five determinants: frequency or pitch, amplitude or loudness, overtone structure or timbre, duration, and morphology (how the sound begins, goes on, and dies away). By the alteration of any one of these

determinants, the position of the sound in sound space changes. Any sound at any point in this total sound space can move to become a sound at any other point.[19]

Needless to say, Cage's 'determinants' are what I've called musical variables, of which 'amplitude' is volume and the 'morphology' he mentions would probably be described as a sound's envelope today.[20] We see that Cage is somewhat sonocentric, too – as its name makes obvious, his 'sound space' doesn't take any non-sonic variables into account, which is why I prefer to imagine a broader 'music space'. On the other hand, Cage's sound space does timbre take into account, thus recognising that frequency, volume and time can be 'built up into' the variable of timbre, perhaps for the sake of convenience.

Cage's sound space is effectively a map of musical possibility. It enables us to easily imagine all the ways in which sounds can change and what forms they can take at the point of the performance event. We can imagine all possible sounds (i.e. performance events) existing within sound space side by side as in an abstract, impeccably organised and virtually infinite library, waiting for selection by browsing composers. As such, sound space can be thought of as a *set of all possible sounds* – we can think of the word 'set' in its mathematical sense (a set of numbers satisfying a certain condition, for example), or in a more everyday sense, as with a 'complete set' of all books, say, by a certain author. As an abstract 'complete set' of all possible sounds, sound space can be used both as a way of *composing* new sounds and *describing* sounds that already exist. It provides a *system* for creating sounds and 'cataloguing' their attributes, 'understanding' them as a structure of certain variables and values, even 'analysing' them according to a prescribed structure of variabilities.

Cage's sound space system can theoretically compose or describe a vast number of different sounds and was daringly broad for its time. Even today, over fifty years later, both acoustic and electronic composers often seem unaware of all the possibilities that Cage envisioned, and constantly retreat to formal conventions derived from the acoustic music of the past. Many seem not to have noticed how vast the possibilities of sound space are, and check out the same few well-worn books from its library over and over again (granted, they may be great books, 'the classics'). A system like sound space remedies this, and helps the imaginations of composers to take flight. We could call it an *imagining system*, or more specifically, a *composing system*.

Note, too, how Cage realises that any sound within the space can be seamlessly transformed into any other through any alteration of their determinants, making all the sounds within it continuous with each other (i.e. they can form a continuum), and his usage of technical terminology such as 'amplitude' implies that the 'determinants' are to be considered continuous variables. Sounds can move continuously, seamlessly through sound space without having to leap across to any discrete 'steps'. In fact later in the same lecture, Cage had this to say about what I've referred to as quantisation:

> Musical habits include scales, modes, theories of counterpoint and harmony, and the study of the timbres... In mathematical terms these all concern discrete steps. They resemble walking – in the case of pitches, on stepping-stones twelve in number. This cautious stepping is not characteristic of the possibilities of magnetic tape, which is revealing to us that musical action or existence can occur at any point or along any line or curve or what have you in total sound space; that we are, in fact, technically equipped to transform our contemporary awareness of nature's manner of operation into art.[21]

By arguing that composers should return to continuous values and not the seemingly discrete conceptual structures we habitually use, Cage clearly believed in what at the end of Part 1 I called 'dequantisation'.

Recognising Variables

Cage's use of certain variables to describe his sound space (and not others, such as non-sonic variables) is a clear example of Part 1's running theme of '(not) taking musical variables into account within a context'. Cage's sound space is both a 'context' for sound-making and an 'account of it', and it's a context in which only certain variables that can determine that sound are taken into that account, or are 'noticed' or 'registered' within that account. As such, we could say that Cage's *system* only *recognises* certain variables. From now on, I'll refer to this idea of 'taking certain variables into account within a musical context' as *recognising certain variables within a system*.

Cage's sound space system can be used to both compose and describe musical objects such as sounds, but *only as long as those musical objects don't include variables or values that the system doesn't recognise*. For example, let's imagine a musical object that Cage's system may not be able to recognise: a constant drone that alternates between two speakers in stereo, arranged so that one speaker is to the left of the listeners and one is to the right. Cage's system does not take into account – does not recognise – any variables that describe the direction a sound might be coming from, so while it would be able to recognise the constant drone, it would not recognise its passing between the two speakers. Thus Cage's system effectively listens to (recognises) sounds in 'mono', and it wouldn't be able to compose or describe musical objects as they exist in stereo. Maybe Cage considered the direction of a sound relative to a listener to be a non-sonic variable, but in any case it's a variable that applies at a greater degree of specification than Cage's system recognises and in the age of stereo speakers it's a variable that practically all modern concrete composers pay close attention to. We can forgive this of

Cage in 1957 before stereo became commonplace, but evidently any idea of 'music space' must improve on Cage's sound space by being able to recognise more variables than his system allowed for. So even though it was very large (indeed, practically infinite), it turns out that Cage didn't provide composers with 'the complete set' of all possible sounds after all.

Similarly, it's not just variables themselves that Cage's system can't recognise. It can't recognise any sounds incorporating values beyond the limited range imposed on its variables either. That range was everything that an ear can determine, so Cage's sound space effectively listens to sounds with an ear, one that we might presume belongs to a human. This isn't so much of an oversight, perhaps – at least not unless we consider the ultrasonic communications of bats and rodents to be music for humans to appreciate as such, or until human ears can be augmented, or radio waves can be beamed directly into a receiver connected to the human brain that can convey to that brain a wider range of frequencies. More prosaically though, it's simply the case that different ears, human or otherwise, have different hearing abilities. Furthermore, since the nineteen-fifties it's become difficult in the field of neuroscience to separate the ear and the brain in the activity of 'determining' sound. Put simply, just like the eye receives light, the ear receives sounds, and the brain then makes some sense of them.

Constituting Musical Objects

So since it only recognises certain variables and values, there are some musical objects that Cage's sound space system is unable to compose or describe. I will refer to a system's dual activity of 'composing' and 'describing' musical objects as *constituting* them, because the two are often not strictly separate activities – they both, in a certain sense, bring a musical object into 'being'. The verbs 'recognising', 'imagining', 'creating', 'composing', 'listening', 'describing', 'defining', 'specifying' and 'constituting' are all just different linguistic facets of what is ultimately the same process: that of the construction or reconstruction of some specific musical attributes. Cage's system, for example, cannot constitute a sound that alternates between two (or more) speakers, or a sound with ultrasonic frequencies – it cannot compose or describe it. So we can sum up thus: *systems of variables constitute musical objects*. And more basically, *variables and values constitute music*.

Here you may begin to notice a certain symmetry in the above statement that might seem rather confusing, but it is deliberate. If systems of variables constitute musical objects, does it work the other way around – do musical objects constitute systems of variables? Of course they do, because what was Cage's sound space, if not a musical object itself? Like any musical object, Cage's sound space is a configuration of musical variables with ranges imposed on them. As such it's very much like a musical work, instrument or style, because it's a specific set of constraints on the variability of sound, a locus. It's a very flexible musical object, too, because it can constitute or actualise an enormous array of possible performance events. In fact, as we can see from how Cage introduced the concept, if sound space were a musical instrument then it would effectively be that newly invented tape recorder, with its much broader potential to manipulate sounds. Also like an instrument or a style, it doesn't set up one single finite time continuum in which all those sounds must exist, though we can interpret Cage's use of the word 'duration' to refer both to the durations of discrete sounds and to durations that span a collection of discrete sounds (the latter being what I've called 'time continuums'). A musical object, then, *is* a constrained system of musical variables, and a constrained system of musical variables is a musical object.

These systems recognise, compose and describe certain variables and certain values. We could say that they're 'composed of' (constituted by) those variables and those constraints, just as a musical object is 'composed of' (constituted by) certain variables and certain constraints on them. Let's take a musical object as an example: the piano. We saw some of the constraints imposed on musical variability represented by the piano in Part 1. Its pitch variable is quantised to equally tempered keys, which are limited to a range of typically eighty-eight in number. Within these constraints, a piano can constitute a great range of sounds (or more accurately, a range of musical objects). As such we could certainly say that like Cage's sound space, a piano is a 'composing system' or an 'imagining system' for constituting musical objects. But as a system, a piano cannot 'recognise' or constitute pitches that might lie 'between' its discrete keys or outside of its ranges. Nor can it constitute sounds that have different timbres, which would lie outside of its timbre range.

If the systems I've alluded to above amount to musical objects then it means, somewhat counter-intuitively, that musical objects can in turn recognise, compose (i.e. create) and *describe* other systems of variables. A musical object is not just a composing or imagining system, it's also a *describing system*. A describing system would detail how a given other musical object is analysed or listened to, and so requires another different musical object that the describing system would analyse (or 'recompose') rather than composing sounds from scratch. Our concern here is primarily with the composition of music, not its description and analysis, but we can briefly consider how a musical object might 'describe' a pre-existing sound. This would essentially entail the musical object being 'fed into' a pre-existing musical object which then 'recreates', 're-describes' or *reconstitutes* it imperfectly, reflecting it in the mirror of its own specific abilities as a describing system. This is comparable to feeding a picture into a photocopier, which converts its colours and subtle shades into a black-and-white description, or how a group of people, with all their many complexities, can be reduced to and described as a specific statistical model.

68

Let's return to the system (musical object) that is the piano. If we 'fed' a descending slide played on a trombone (i.e. a continuously descending pitch) into a piano, the piano wouldn't be able to recognise the pitches 'in between' its own keys, and so it would constitute that musical object as a descending run of discrete scale notes. A piano wouldn't be able to constitute the trombone's timbre values either, and would instead substitute its own. The trombone slide would effectively be quantised or 'bottlenecked' into what the piano system allows. We could imagine a more complex example, too: we could 'feed' human speech into a piano. Human speech is a complex series of continuously varying pitches, timbres and volumes, but a piano would only be able to reconstitute it as a bewildering series of dissonant notes and intervals arranged in highly subtle rhythmic framework.[22] Of course, using musical objects as describing systems to imperfectly reconstitute other musical objects is a rich vein for compositional experiment.

Similarly, we could imagine an old or otherwise low quality tape recorder as an example of a musical object that could also be a system for describing musical objects. We can 'feed' sounds into a tape recorder (i.e. record them), and when the tape recorder plays them back they come back reconstituted through the tape recorder's system of constrained variables. Sounds recorded onto a tape recorder will never come back exactly the same, of course, which may be because of the limited abilities of the tape to store the sound or the speaker(s) to play back the sound. This is where the term 'fidelity', in this case fidelity to the original musical object, is used in music technology. 'Hi-fi' is short for 'high fidelity', but no fidelity is perfect. The opposite term 'lo-fi' has recently gained currency and is often used to describe music that is 'reconstituted' through something like an old or low quality tape recorder. Lo-fi tape recorders are often unable to reconstitute fairly high or very low frequencies in musical objects at the original volume or even at all. In playing back the sounds through lo-fi speakers, the musical object may also acquire a certain amount of distortion.

We could say that in reconstituting the musical object with a certain deficiency in fidelity, a tape recorder will leave a 'signature' or 'imprint' on the original musical object, which in the case of certain variables (such as volume and frequency) has a *negative effect* on the original values. This 'imprint' is a musical object itself of course (remember that musical objects don't have to actually make a sound in themselves, that is, they don't have to have any specific timbre variables to produce that sound. All sounds are musical objects, but not all musical objects are 'sounds'.[23])

This is an example of the values of variables in a musical object (the 'imprint') being *negative* – those of frequency and volume were negative, their values were negative numbers. This means, of course, that they require another at least partly positive prior 'host' musical object to have any effect in actual performance. We could say that the musical object that is the tape recorder's imprint is 'added to' the original sound, since to add negative values is to reduce positive values. We're not simply adding the tape recorder to the original musical object, otherwise both would be performing at the same time – we're using the 'imprint' of the tape recorder to modify the original musical object.

Subsets, Subspaces, Concentric Musical Objects

If the musical object that is Cage's sound space is a set or system of all possible sounds that can be constituted within its particular systemic constraints, and if those sounds, because they are musical objects themselves, are in turn systems of variables, then we can see how *musical objects are subsets of music space*. The piano system discussed earlier is a musical object, and it's a subset of Cage's sound space because it represents a narrower, more constrained range of possibilities *within* Cage's sound space system. We could think of the piano system as a 'piano space', a *subspace* of Cage's sound space. The set of all possible sounds in a piano space will naturally be smaller than the set of all possible sounds in a 'total sound space', which will contain all the sounds of piano space because it contains all possible sounds within it.

Musical objects are subsets or subspaces within music space. Let's remind ourselves: what do these sets and subsets *contain*? Remember that a flexible musical object can give rise to many different performance events: it is a space in which multiple different performance events are made possible, and it can actualise as any of those performance events. If a musical object is a set or space, then that set or space contains the full range of possible performance events that that musical object can actualise. To continue the analogy of sound space as a library of all possible books, a musical object is like a subsection of that library, containing books limited to a particular range of attributes. If that musical object can actualise more than one different performance, then it's flexible. If that musical object can only actualise a single, infinitely specific performance event, then it's 'concrete'. Each of the performance events that a flexible musical object can actualise is a single, infinitely specific point located in the space represented by that musical object, each of which in turn can be thought of as a 'concrete' musical object. To create a subset or subspace is to constrain the performance possibilities of the larger space it's contained within in a certain way, and that constraining is determined by the variables and the constraints on them that make up that subspace, that musical object.

Conversely, a notionally 'concrete' musical object is just one single, infinitely specific location within the space described by a musical object. Because it's concrete it has no space in which to differ, no moving parts, no room to move within the system that constitutes it. This is the case even within the loci of time variables: a truly concrete musical object is a single, frozen, infinitely specified instant in time rather than something that differs in time (here, we will generally be assuming, for the sake of simplicity, that they can). Remember, though, that a concrete musical object can only be concrete if we don't take any of those variables through which it may differ in actual performance into account. In the terms I've used previously, a concrete musical object must be constituted by or in the context of – or 'concrete to' – a particular system. 'Concrete' is a relative term that depends on the abilities of a system that constitutes it, and the only way a musical object can be as concrete as possible is if the system that constitutes it is the entire physically constrained universe itself, which would leave no further possible values of variables to be specified. Composers can get very close to concreteness, but they can never truly reach absolute concreteness unless they happen to be in complete control of values for every single kind of change within the universe's constrained system, including the attributes of every particle, and so on.

We can imagine, then, musical objects as a series of subsets of larger, preceding sets, that get smaller and smaller right down to that notional point of the single concrete, infinitely specific performance event. These musical objects would be arranged *concentrically*, rather like Russian dolls that contain within them a series of increasingly small 'sub-dolls' (although this analogy can't allow for how we may take any path we like in limiting the range of each subset, not just a simple linear one as is the case with the dolls). We can start with a 'piano space' contained within music space: piano space is a subset of music space, and in turn a scale of A major played on a piano is a subset of piano space, the scale of A major starting at A4 played on a piano is a subset of that musical object, an A4 played alone on a piano is a subset of that musical object, and A4 played on a piano for four seconds is a subset of that (any of these musical objects could be members of other sets, of course, such as the set of all A major scales on any instruments). Eventually, after sufficiently high or infinite series of subsets, we'd have a single infinitely specific concrete musical object, an unrepeatable performance event like the river we can't ❧ step into twice: something like 'A4 played on a piano for four seconds at 4:38pm and twenty-two seconds on the 10th of September 2010, heard from three metres away by the ears of Person x, which are...' and so on, yet infinitely specific with regard to the values of any and all possible musical variables relating to that performance event (such as those relating to the positions and momentums of all the air molecules conveying the sound, for example).

Let's have another example, this time considering a musical object we might call a 'style'. Remember that the values and variables that make up styles as musical objects would be statistically derived from a sample of relevant performance events. As musical objects, they're 'fuzzy' – their constraints aren't as clear-cut as those of a particular instrument or digital sound file, for example. Most of the musical objects we refer to have some degree of this statistical fuzziness, but styles are such broad and complex entities, encompassing millions upon millions of potential variables and values, that we can only really speak of averages, correlations, probabilities and emerging patterns within the music's variability. But even if we can't precisely define the borders and structures of a particular 'style space x', styles are no less musical objects for that.

The concept of 'jazz music' is sometimes considered to be too large to be described by the word 'style'. It could also be called a 'genre', a 'tradition' or 'a music', but we can consider it a style, albeit one at a larger scale, one with a greater locus of difference. 'Jazz space' is a subset of music space containing all possible performance events we would consider definable as 'jazz' (this also includes the playing of jazz recordings.) This is a space of all jazz: past, present, future and all jazz performances that may never be actualised.

Note that the word 'jazz' is the weak link here, its semantic ambiguity giving it a capacity for disagreement and making it a rather arbitrary criterion for defining this space's contents. How would you describe the details of a 'jazz performance' taking place at some distant point in the future? You can't, of course – 'jazz' is just a word, a label. A more rigorous conceptual definition could be created for the 'jazz' contained within 'jazz space', perhaps stipulating certain instruments, the element of improvisation and so on. If that definition was a system of constrained variables, we could calculate statistically how close a given musical object (once constituted using the same system of variables) was to that definition, and thus how appropriate the term 'jazz' is to that object, perhaps given as a percentage. But this definition could either be too vague, too limiting or simply incorrect in the opinions of others. An exhaustive statistical account of the characteristics of 'jazz' up to the present point in history could be created, but it would only have a limited ability to show what new kinds of performance events definable as 'jazz' could be developed in the future. Besides, it would still have had to be derived from finite data selected because it was thought to have something to do with the word 'jazz' or a definition thereof. Or we could somehow statistically analyse all music to see if some performances conformed to a correlation that we might infer to be what we'd called 'jazz' all along – a correlation which is quite probably there to be found. But in order to do this, we'd have to define music too. And this same linguistic problem applies to the word 'music', of course, further underlying that music is continuous with life and the universe, being just a vaguely defined area within it rather than an absolutely discrete entity.

But what's important here aren't the precise definitions of the contents of musical objects as sets, but the workings of a system of concentric musical objects constituted by increasingly constrained variables. 'Jazz' may not be exhaustively definable, but it's still a musical object we can discuss practically. A subset of jazz space might be 'jazz after the end of the Second World War', a category whose contents are constrained to certain values of historical date. A subset of this might be 'the jazz music of Miles Davis', and a subset of that could be 'the jazz music of Miles Davis considered to be in the style called cool jazz'. We can imagine a 'cool jazz space', too, including the work of other musicians associated with the style. Contained within the 'Miles Davis's cool jazz' subset would be his concert of February 12th 1964 at the Philharmonic Hall of Lincoln Center, New York. This concert was recorded and released under the title *My Funny Valentine*, a recording which is contained within the 'Miles Davis's cool jazz' set just like the concert. That concert is indeed a performance event, but it'd be a flexible subset too if you think about it, because at every different point in the concert hall and at every instant within the time of the performance, the sounds to be heard were slightly different. This last may seem like a fatuous point from a practical point of view, but it does show how, *in actuality*, concrete musical events are infinitely specified, such that one cannot experience ('step into') the same performance – the same concrete musical object – twice. Jazz space is made up of these infinitely specific 'jazz events', from which the flexible subsets of musical objects described above are abstractions.

One more example, so as to further illustrate these ideas and show how all musical objects are equivalent in kind. This time let's take a musical work, a song: 'Behind the Mask', originally written and released by the electropop band Yellow Magic Orchestra as a single in 1980. As a musical object it's a set of all possible actualisations of that song. Again, the definition is not precise. This set contains all recordings of the song performed by Yellow Magic Orchestra. It also contains all performances of the revised version released by band member Ryuichi Sakamoto in 1987 and those of the cover versions by Eric Clapton and Greg Phillinganes too. In fact, it contains all possible 'versions' of that song, whether they've actually been performed (actualised) to date or not. We can't precisely define what the criteria for a version of the song are – we could even imagine composers producing something that sounds nothing like the 'original', and yet claiming it to be a cover version of the song, and it could be appreciated ironically or metaphorically, perhaps.

The chorus of 'Behind the Mask' is a subset of the song, as is just the first iteration of the chorus, each verse, the song's main riff throughout, the song's main riff just in the opening four bars, and all the constituent parts of the song, constituted in every way. Of course, as these constituent parts become more specific, they'll differ from cover version to cover version. And what if Yellow Magic Orchestra performed the song and one of the players accidentally missed out or misplayed some of its notes? We might say that this was still an actualisation of the song. In fact, we can proceed continuously to more problematic performances, from this negligible scenario to one in which the performance was a complete disaster – all the band members are somehow drugged and fall unconscious ten seconds into the song, nose-diving into their equipment, producing a chaotic sound followed by the constant drone of depressed synthesiser keys. Again, this leaves us feeling the need to draw some dividing line around what constitutes a performance of the song, which would only be arbitrary and rather weak. And again, we'd need statistical analysis to reduce the problem to one of probabilities clustering around some derived average performance. The musical objects that we infer from the real world are statistically derived, and have problematic, imprecise relationships to the words we use to represent them. This concerns musical analysts far more than composers, of course, unless the latter wish to research music in order to produce music that was consistent (or inconsistent) with statistics about other music.

Hopefully all this further illustrates why individual 'sounds' are difficult to pin down as coherent, conceptual entities and an insufficient basis on which to think of musical possibilities. Sounds and all those other musical structures we wouldn't conventionally call a 'sound' (e.g. pure rhythm) are all musical objects and can be arranged in complicated, concentric interrelationships as subsets of music space. Musical works are musical objects, for example, and they can be divided up into any number of subsets or musical sub-objects that aren't reducible to the concept of fixed, discrete 'sounds'. Less conventionally, we can divide up instruments and styles into musical sub-objects (all the pitches below 440Hz on a guitar, for example), and any other flexible musical object too.

In fact, we can think of Cage's sound space as a subset or subspace of the broader 'music space' concept. Naturally, this means that music space itself is a musical object, the most flexible musical object possible. It's Music itself, of course, in its rawest sense. If music space were presented as a musical work to a performer, it would simply be an instruction to 'produce what may be considered to be music: any time, any way and in any circumstances'. As a system, such a musical work would be able to constitute a virtually infinite number of performance events.

Dimensions in Sound Space

What sort of a space is Cage's sound space? He doesn't really discuss quite how sounds might move through it. Put simply, when objects move through conventional physical space they move through three *dimensions*. In some cases we can also say there's a dimension of time: for example, even if an object is not moving in any of the three spatial dimensions, it is nonetheless being moved forward in time. These dimensions can be thought of as variables giving continuous spatial values between 'left and right' (first dimension), 'up and down' (second dimension), 'forward and backward' (third dimension) and 'earlier and later' (time dimension). In maths, science and statistics, the relationships between variables and their values are demonstrated in exactly this way on graphs. Each variable is assigned to a dimension (that is, an axis on the graph) and the values given by those variables are plotted as single points in the resulting space where those variables coincide. Once plotted, these points can be connected by lines or curves. So effectively, Cage's sound space is a graph on which sounds can be plotted as single points or as a series of connected points.

Often when sound waves are visualised on a computer they're plotted on graphs as curves of varying volume over time, because volume (given by the amplitude of the sound wave) corresponds to the voltage that controls how hard the computer's speakers will shift air, creating the force of air on an eardrum or other receiver that makes up sound. Pitch (i.e. frequency) results from the speed at which that volume is oscillating as amplitude in time, so it isn't necessary to include an axis of pitch, and the same applies to all other sonic variables.[24] This space has only two variables, two dimensions, and yet it can reproduce sound with a high fidelity – as much fidelity as the computer's capabilities allow (i.e. as much as the computer as system can constitute). Just as texture and timbre can be 'broken down' into more basic variables, so all sonic variables can – assuming there's a medium for the sound waves to propagate through, namely air – in turn be 'broken down' into amplitude and time.[25] Since it's practically impossible for composers to be able to limit their decision-making to just those two variables, they 'build up' higher structures such as texture and timbre and use those as variables whose values are quantised to a choice of pre-established 'multivariate' structures (i.e. musical objects comprising more than one variable). Similarly, even higher structures can be among the options opened up by variables, as was the case with the 'preset reverb or not' variable and the variable of timbre as quantised to a range of pre-established classical instruments discussed in Part 1.

Because it recognises five variables, then, Cage's sound space is effectively a five-dimensional space. He might not have mentioned this because he realised that timbre and 'morphology' were in fact multidimensional, composite variables as discussed earlier, but he may also have wanted to avoid confusing and distracting his audience. It's easy to imagine a single point in any dimensionality, but it's difficult to imagine something moving continuously through five dimensions. Doing so isn't strictly necessary, of course, as we only need to remember that there are five notionally independent ways in which sounds can vary in Cage's system. Borrowing a term from science and statistics that we'll return to later, we could say that the sounds in Cage's sound space have five *degrees of freedom*.

In many areas of science, particularly dynamical systems theory, a system like Cage's sound space can be depicted as a 'phase space' or 'state space'. [26] Any configuration of the values of those variables, and thus *any possible state of a system*, can be represented by a single point plotted, as on a graph, in that system's phase space. A phase space describes a system by constituting every possible state in which the system can be presented regarding any and all possible combinations of the values given by those variables. A pendulum, for example, is a system that passes through multiple spatial positions and amounts of momentum while in motion, so the variables of 'position in one spatial dimension' and 'momentum' form the dimensions that are used to mark all the possible states of that system as points in a two-dimensional phase space.

Phase spaces constitute a particular identity for the system, and will only recognise certain variables of the system in doing so. A pendulum's two-dimensional phase space does not recognise any variables that would constitute the colour of the pendulum, for example: its colour is an attribute of the pendulum system that will not change and is considered irrelevant to its identity as depicted in the two-dimensional phase space. It's not an aspect of the particular identity the phase space constitutes as a system – the phase space constitutes a pendulum, not a pendulum of any particular colour. So a phase space is a way of constituting a system or object with regard to certain variables, showing how it can exist in various states *while retaining some particular unified* or *grouped identity* as a system or object, *whatever else may change*, whatever the values of any and all other potential variables (colour, location etc.) may be.[27]

Cage's sound space is an attempt at creating a phase space for, as he called it, 'the entire field of sound'.[28] Each of the points in Cage's sound space is a possible state that the sound space as system can actualise, that is, a possible concrete performance event that that system can constitute. Similarly, every musical object is a multidimensional and constrained subspace – a phase space – of that possibility, with each of the points in that phase space corresponding to a possible performance event that the musical object can constitute. Put simply then, flexible musical objects are graphs or particular sets of points on a graph, with certain variables marking the dimensions, which create a space in which all the performance events that that musical object can constitute can be plotted as single points (if relatively concrete, i.e. 'concrete to' that musical object) or collections of points (if flexible, which strictly speaking includes flexibility in time). Subsets or subspaces of those musical objects (which are themselves musical objects, sub-objects) represent particular, more specific areas within those graphs.

Dimensions in Music Space

The music space I refer to here is a larger space of possibility than Cage's sound space. Music space must be able to encompass as many musical variables and values as anyone could possibly need to constitute a musical object, however complicated that musical object is. Because of this it's a highly multidimensional space in which any possible musical performance whatsoever – from just one note played on an instrument to an entire orchestral concert – can conceivably be represented as a single point, that is, constituted using a system of variables, as concrete to that system.[29]

According to our definition of music in Part 1, music space is a notional phase space that can constitute all possible art objects (i.e. collections of performance events) that relate primarily to the production of sound as a single point, whatever variables they include. Thus its borders are only 'what is considered to be music', according to that or whatever other definition. As previously discussed, music space can actually be thought of as continuous with art and life in general, bleeding into it and not absolutely discrete from it, so there's no way, reason or need to draw an absolute perimeter around 'musical activity' for the purposes of compositional possibility, much less dig a conceptual moat.

Because it can draw on so many different variables – as many variables as we might consider necessary to compose music – music space's dimensionality must therefore effectively vary depending on what dimensions are required to constitute the variable structures of any possible musical object and consequently any possible performance event. In short, not all musical objects are specifically composed of the same set of variables, unlike the sounds in Cage's sound space. We've seen that variables, their values and the musical objects they constitute are not so simple and absolute: they can be 'built up' and 'broken down' into concentric structures that then become values for other 'bigger' or 'smaller' variables. This process is comparable to how interactions between forces go into creating structures at different scales – subatomic particles, then atoms, molecules, cells, organisms, and so on. In the same way, music space must be able to recognise variables and values at any and every scale of music-making, whether it be the tuning of a single note, the harmonic structure used in a musical work or the choice of which entire musical work is to be played during a concert, because composers and listener are able to recognise variables at any such scale, and any of them could be important to music.

This means that music space must be able to account for how the same variables can apply within a musical object in different ways, at different stages and over any area of that object, and can recur at multiple different points in that musical object. For example, it rarely makes sense to think of a musical work as having one single pitch variable that changes its values throughout. Even if this could technically be done in Cage's sound space, musical works can be said to feature multiple pitch variables applying at different points throughout the duration of the work: variables of 'pitch of instrument a', 'pitch of instrument b', and even 'first pitch', 'second pitch' and so on. This is how, as I touched upon in Part 1, a musical object could potentially be constituted using a system of a virtually infinite number of variables applying in a virtually infinite number of orders or other interrelationships. If it's going to compose or describe a musical work with at least two separate instruments or two separate notes, music space may need more than the one single dimension of pitch Cage's sound space had. Thus because of all the different and complex dimensionalities that musical objects may have, music space can't have one fixed number of variables to act as dimensions in the space, unlike Cage's sound space. It can't have one absolute set of axes – it can't be depicted as a single, typical graph, however many dimensions that graph may depict.

To illustrate this point, we can return to the idea discussed earlier of musical objects acting as describing systems and 'reconstituting' other musical objects (the sliding, talking piano, the old tape recorder). The higher the number and complexity of variables used to constitute a musical object, the more difficult it will become to use the exact same system (i.e. the same kind of graph) to describe a very similar musical object in a suitable amount of detail. Take five minutes of modern concrete music as an example of a particularly complex musical object: so many attributes can be varied in so many ways and at so many points that if a system were devised that could constitute the piece to a high degree of specificity (say, the level of specificity that a closely attentive human listener might perceive), it would be so complex that it would probably be impossible to use that very same system (same axes) to describe a different musical work of similar complexity with any sufficient fidelity.

This means that in order to constitute a musical object using music space, we must effectively 'select' or specify a certain finite number of dimensions that will define its particular 'space' and ignore the rest of the infinite possible variables in music space as being not applicable to that musical object's identity. Music space is a relativistic version of Cage's sound space, it's created from scratch according to the increasing complexity of the musical objects making it up (we'll discuss this later on as *the progressive specification of music space*), rather than referring back to and being defined through one prior and absolute set of axes. In other words, we must create our own 'temporary', impermanent graphs for them, choosing the dimensions and the ranges of the points within them ourselves, rather than relying on the static dimensionality of a single given system. Because they won't recognise certain variables, these graphs will only be able to constitute performance events in a limited way, but this needn't worry composers as long as the infinite potential of music space from which these musical objects arose is borne in mind. Musical objects, with their limited potential for composing or describing sounds, are what composers work with, and have been working with since music began. Let's focus on musical objects and their properties and uses before we go any further into the nature of music space.

Using Musical Objects

Musical objects are the *dramatis personae* of music. But they are not objects in an everyday sense. They aren't always 'sounds' in the normal sense of the word – a musical object doesn't require any directly sound-making variables, it could have aspects of 'pure rhythm' without pitch, or 'pure pitch' without timbre, for example. The alternation between two speakers we considered earlier, for example, is a musical object in itself regardless of any particular attributes of the sounds coming out of them – those attributes being values given by variables outside of and thus irrelevant to that stereo alternation's defined identity as a musical object. Besides, especially in composition, 'sounds' tend to be conventionally thought of as particular, discrete performance events rather than more flexible musical objects that can be actualised in a certain range of different concrete performance events.

But nor are many musical objects really 'things' in the immediately traditional sense. Musical objects are *abstractions*: they are collections of certain possible performance events grouped together as a certain limited identity defined by a certain set of constrained variables, and abstracted – extrapolated – from actual, concrete reality. Returning to Heraclitus's saying, 'one cannot step twice into the same river', we can say that in parallel, one cannot experience the same actualised musical performance twice, but there can be the conceptual object or phase space of 'a river' or 'the river' that remains, even though that river is always actualised ('performed') differently. Musical objects remain, as abstract concepts, in the same way. We can't step twice into the same music, but if we unify a range of musical events as a constrained locus of variability, we can at least step into the same musical object twice – we can play the clarinet twice, we can see the same musical twice, we can hear rock music twice. But take away the words or conceptual definitions we use to constrain and demarcate their identities, and all such musical objects are continuous with each other, making up the pure variability of music space.

Though I'm treating musical objects as 'things', as nouns, they're really more of a cross between nouns and verbs. Remember that music and everything in it is an event. Musical objects serve to constitute that event and the parts of it to varying degrees of specification. They can even be thought of as adjectives or adverbs, too, because they describe the attributes of that event. But composers can think of musical objects as nouns in a practical sense. Composers invent and use musical objects in the same way that sculptors make sculptures from invented or found objects – by combining them (or to put it a better way, using them on each other) to form a new (musical) object. This is not to say that musical objects already exist, fully specified and constituted, in the minds of composers, to be plucked out and inserted into the music as a neat row of objects. Composition is usually more fluid and intuitive than that. But as an idea, as a way of making sense of musical activity, musical objects – especially in their capacity as 'composing systems' and 'imagining systems' – can indeed give some form and organisation to the process of composition. Like the bitesize versions of music space that they are, they can aid composers' imaginations and in helpfully specific ways too.

How do composers conceptualise, use and combine musical objects? Let's imagine a specific musical object, a specific sort of reverb – the reverb used in a particular rock song in the nineteen-eighties, say (reverb was often heavily applied to rock songs at the time). Note that reverb as a musical object doesn't make a sound in itself, but that doesn't matter, it just means we have to apply it to another musical object that will create a sound for it to have any actual effect. Lots of musical objects have names with differing degrees of precision, but most of them don't; let's give that musical object an arbitrary (and by no means uniquely identifying) name: 'eighties rock reverb'. So here we're thinking of it as a noun: *that eighties rock reverb*. But we can also think of it as a verb, an action, in that we can apply it to another musical object – we may have four bars of a particular guitar solo that *does* include a timbre variable and we could put that reverb 'on' it or 'apply that reverb to it'. As a system with a certain identity, those four bars of guitar solo didn't have any variables describing the reverb as dimensions in their phase space. Once we applied the eighties rock reverb we created a new, more specific musical object ('four bars of guitar solo *with* that eighties rock reverb on it') that is both a subset of the eighties rock reverb as musical object *and* a subset of the four bars of guitar solo.

This may seem a confusing outcome, but remember that this new musical object and all its possible actualisations in performance were already potential actualisations in performance of both its two 'parent' musical objects. What's been done by combining the two musical objects is the same as what happens when two circles (i.e. sets) are intersected on a Venn diagram. That eighties rock reverb would remain the same musical object whatever other musical object it was applied to (unless something in that second musical object interfered with the identity of that musical object – by having negative values given by reverb variables, for example). In the same way, the four bars of guitar solo are the same musical object whether there's reverb on them or not. Similarly that 'child' musical object ('four bars of guitar solo *with* that eighties rock reverb on it') will remain the same as a concept whichever other variables come into it – it'll be the same concept whether it plays out of a left or a right speaker for example. It wouldn't be the same actualised performance event (the 'same river') if it were to play out of different speakers, but we would be able to say that it's the same musical object ('*a* river') in both cases.

A musical object represents a certain constrained locus of musical possibilities, but of course, there's no way of telling as a listener what particular musical object's locus something in the music 'came from'. Music is a stream of information that cannot somehow 'truly' betray the real musical objects that were 'in the minds' of the composers, though some guesses as to this can be more accurate than others. As a musical 'text', we can divide or differentiate a musical performance into different musical objects in any number of ways. But doing this in some absolute way really isn't necessary for listening, and composers only rarely have a specific sense of what discrete musical objects their music is constructed from. However, a certain impression (i.e. not an exhaustive description of that musical object's identity) of the specific traits of a particular musical object can become familiar with listeners when its effects repeat themselves, especially over time, as we'll see in more detail in Part 3. We come to know musical objects – whether they're musical works, instruments, styles, musical fragments or something else – because they recur, and that's how listeners begin to perceive and appreciate musical objects.

The Infinite Variety of Musical Objects

Within the virtual infinity of music space, musical objects naturally come in all shapes and sizes. A single pitch is a musical object: 440Hz, for example, is a constrained pitch variable that remains the same whatever the values of any other variables might be. Another way to think of it is as a musical object that comprises all the potential variables in music space, but only the variable of pitch is assigned (constrained to) a particular value, so those other variables are merely implied and can be discounted from its identity as a musical object. This pitch is both a 'thing' (a noun), and it gives rise to an action or event (a verb), and it's a musical description (an adjective). We could depict this musical object on a one-dimensional graph, as a line representing the hertz scale on which the 440Hz point is marked. Or we could imagine it as a two-dimensional graph with pitch in Hz on the y axis and all other variables implied along the x axis (but not actually being part of the musical object's defined identity). It would be represented by a horizontal line along the

440 mark on the *y* axis.

Similarly, a timbre is a musical object, whether we precisely define it using synthesiser settings (or some other set of constrained variables) specifying waveforms or whether we simply give it a vague linguistic definition, like 'harsh', whose effects in actual musical performance could be determined statistically, perhaps. A volume of 20dB is a musical object, but so is the idea of 'loudness'. Note that '20dB' is a precise numerical quantity, while values like 'harsh' and 'loud' are merely relative and unmeasured words (which is not at all to say that they're musical objects any less, they're simply more flexible). The instruction to 'play music for twenty seconds' is a musical object, it equates to music lasting for a duration of twenty seconds. The specific details of the music other than its duration don't come into it – it doesn't matter to the identity of the musical object what music is played during those twenty seconds. These are all examples of very simple musical objects, and are easily defined through stipulating variables and constrained values for them.

From these simple beginnings, all musical objects can be built up with increasing complexity. We can define a musical object with two variables as a point or area on a two-dimensional graph: a pitch of 440Hz and the timbre of a violin, or a volume of between 15dB and 30dB and a duration of between twenty and forty minutes. Three variables: a volume between 15dB and 30dB, a pitch of A flat and a duration of semibreve, and so on (note here that unlike the volume variable, the pitch and duration are quantised to the conventions of notation, with the latter being a temporally relative term) and so on. We could even create a musical object from a mixture of sonic and non-sonic variables: a 'warm' timbre, a volume that can vary between *'piano'* and *'mezzo piano'*, a pitch range of C2 to C4, in a major key, to be performed in a corner of London Bridge Station on a rainy day by someone dressed in black. Even these fairly simple lists of variables and the constraints on them can start to become interesting musical 'art' objects in themselves, in much the same way that musical works, styles and instruments can be. Imagine the different ways in which such a musical object could be actualised or 'interpreted' in performance, in the same way that performers interpret musical works or instruments, or composers give their own interpretation of a musical style. Remember that 'works', 'instruments' and 'styles' are all equivalent in being musical objects and are just different linguistic-conceptual facets of the same continuum of musical variability. The set of variables described above could be thought of as being in any of the three categories, but really there isn't yet a practical name for the sort of musical object it is.

As touched upon earlier, a musical object may have multiple areas within it defined by the same type of variable. It could have 'first pitch' and 'second pitch' variables, each perhaps with further constrained variables on them, such as volume or position within time continuums. Or they could have no necessary order implied, and just be 'pitch a' and 'pitch b', or 'position a' and 'position b'. The values of variables might refer to more complex pre-established or partially pre-established (i.e. flexible) structures: '[which] melody', 'melody 1' and 'melody 2', '[which] texture', 'rhythm a' and 'rhythm b'. We begin to see that if any musical object can itself be given as a value expressed by a particular variable, which can then in turn combine with other variables, music becomes a complex system of all kinds of controlled variability pretty quickly, able to actualise countless numbers of musical performances. In fact, most composers launch into this system already at a stage of some complexity, and compose relatively instinctively, without considering every possible variable – only those they consider relevant to the task in hand.

Imagining these variables and their constraints being added one by one in a continuous process, in any order and in any way, we make up all the musical objects we already have some idea of, even if they could only be imperfectly or statistically defined. It'd be hugely difficult to draw a comprehensive graph representing a musical object as complex as 'jazz' or 'Behind the Mask', of course. For one thing, there are many different ways to divide both into certain relevant variables, to constitute its variability (or 'parameterise' it), especially if the values of variables can express complex multivariate musical objects themselves. This is because there are many different routes through different collections of variables that can achieve the same sonic or musical effect, and it is usually unclear how variables applied, and the relationships between them, how independent or dependent they were on each other and so on. But again, we've strayed into the province of musical analysis here. The point is that this difficulty in pinning down a precise pattern of variability in these more complex musical objects needn't prevent us from imagining them *as* musical objects.

Musical objects can also be entirely non-sonic. The distinctive costumes worn by rock bands such as Devo or Kiss can be said to be musical objects. They are art objects relating primarily to the production of sound, they are a part of the musical experience. Concert halls like the Royal Albert Hall or the Sydney Opera House are musical objects, in certain capacities at least, whose acoustic attributes would also have sonic consequences. You may disagree that a costume or a concert hall is a musical object occupying a place in the same continuum of music space – after all, it does seem an unconventional idea. But such disagreement would only go so far. Music space is a space of all possible music, which under my own particular definition means art objects relating primarily to sound. Beyond that definition, the category of 'art objects' is deliberately ambiguous, as is the property of 'relating primarily to' sound, but it ventures a lot more than just the label 'music' does. If you disagree with this definition, and would prefer something more limited like 'music is structured sound', then Devo's uniforms aren't musical objects and wouldn't be included in music space under your definitions. I choose to include them, others may not, and this isn't a problem because neither music nor music space have absolute, unmoving borders as concepts. It's all relative and 'music' is ultimately just a word, one that hides the fact that the activity we call by that name is continuous with broader life and the universe, rather than separate from it.

Musical objects don't have to represent independent groupings of musical information, they can represent alterations to the values of other musical objects, alterations that occur prior to or during a musical performance. Like the imperfect tape recorder mentioned earlier, which lowered the volumes of the upper frequencies in whatever musical object was 'fed into' it, musical objects can incorporate negative values. More generally, the values that make up musical objects may be added or subtracted from each other in the process of their combination, or be subjected to any other sort of mathematical function. We can imagine musical objects that add 10Hz, that make other musical objects 'louder', that subtract notes from the ends of melodies, or that multiply the length of time durations by two (a process called 'rhythmic augmentation'). A musical object could even change the values of other musical objects into a certain value or set of values as a mathematical function does, or otherwise move them through music space in any way, even through multiple dimensions. Imagine, for example, a musical object that brought all pitches to 440Hz over time, whether those pitches started above or below 440Hz in pitch. Such a musical object could play an important role in a musical work – say, one in which a group of trombonists could pick any note to play, but must slide that note upwards or downwards towards C4 before playing another note, even, perhaps, if they never actually reached it.

Musical objects like these can guide musical change according to certain characteristics in other musical objects. The music produced by Performers A and B in the example in Part 1 was such a musical object, incorporating 'if... then...' instructions. Such musical objects are a lot more difficult to imagine as traditional graphs, but as they become complex systems of instructions concerning the relationship of dependent and independent variables, they'd be more akin to computer programming code. Such flexible musical objects, interacting dependently on particular circumstances, are very unlike the ways we normally imagine consuming music, namely as the fixed and passive experience of a fixed object independent of any conditions or interventions from 'outside' it. They can lead us to imagine music presented as an interactive art work or even as a game, and there's no reason why such interactive musical works couldn't be appreciated as musical works in their own right. Both relatively 'fixed' and more interactive musical objects are loci of variability – the latter are just more obviously so.

Despite all these different forms that musical objects may come in, they do at least have to make sense. In order for a musical object's definition to have any effective meaning – in order for it to constitute a subset of music space – at least one variable must be constrained in some way, otherwise that musical object is indistinguishable from anything else in music space. Variables aren't themselves musical objects, nor, strictly speaking, are their values, that is, their constraints. Musical objects need at least one variable and at least one constraint to have any significance. This is because a variable without a constraint imposed on its values is no different to music space itself – an instruction to play music at any volume is no different to an instruction to play any music whatsoever. And values without variables are just meaningless data, numbers without dimensions. A constrained variable is what makes a musical object – it creates a piece of musical information.

Similarly, a musical object can't be logically paradoxical. For example, a musical work can be between two minutes and three minutes long, or either two or three minutes long, or can be three minutes long with a two minute long subsection, or a two minute part and a three minute part, but the selfsame variable of duration can't be expressed as values of *both* two minutes *and* three minutes at the same time. In the same way, within the system of Western equal temperament, a note can't have a pitch of A4 and a frequency 1000Hz, because pitch and frequency are equivalent, related quantities. The note A4 has a frequency of around 440Hz, so in the case of a pitched note as a musical object, 'frequency' wouldn't properly count as one of the 'all other variables' of music space in which values may differ while that object's identity remains the same.[30]

Having seen quite how multifarious music space and its constituent constrained variables and more complex musical objects are, one concern may have occurred to some readers by this point. If there can conceivably be a single musical variable in music space expressing any and every kind of change in musical information, however complex, however many other variables can together create exactly the same effects, and that can even incorporate linguistic concepts like 'harsh' with vague, fuzzy effects that we would only be able to understand imperfectly or statistically, then doesn't such a system of infinite variables have no grounding, no absolute significance? Wouldn't it be preferable to have one finite set of differentiated fundamental variables to use as a sort of musical toolkit, like Cage's sound space – a periodic table of musical variability – and dispense with all these vague variables like 'harshness', 'reverb *x* on or off' or 'whether it's raining or not' whose effects could probably already be constituted in exactly the same way through other variables – variables that could be given through such a fundamental system?

But here I'm presenting musical variability as relative, not absolute. Its change emerges relative to itself and not according to a prior system of defined types of change. This is especially the case because all composers and listeners take different paths through the creation and perception of music, which is usually through some mediation of those complex pre-existing musical objects and concepts (harshness, reverb etc.), and not (consciously or unconsciously) through reference to the grounding of some absolute system of musical atoms. Music cannot, should not, constitute a single system, but rather an infinite multiplicity of impermanent concentric systems – a system of systems. Music space is a weightless system, not derived from or reducible to one easily definable musical object (except itself, if you permit the paradox). That a single notional musical variable or value, were it to be stumbled upon, could do anything at all – express any change at all, no matter how complex or imprecise in its effects – is not the weakness of infinite variability but its gift to the needs and imaginations of composers and listeners. It multiplies the paths through which musical information can change to the nth degree.

The Progressive Specification of Music Space

To see how music space is created, how it gives rise to its many different musical possibilities, we can imagine it arranged according to the increasingly complex specification of the musical objects that make it up. We can consider how music's space's constituent information is constituted through a process of *progressive specification* as more and more variables are assigned more and more specific ranges of values. This progression amounts to a continuum moving from simple, general, relatively unspecified forms comprising few constrained variables (such as music with only a few pitches, or music where change only occurs at intervals of one second, or music simply specified as being 'loud') towards the richly detailed forms comprising huge numbers of constrained variables that we more often encounter in musical activity (such as music with complex melodic or harmonic behaviour, or music with complex systems of rhythm and inter-relational durations, or music with a complex structure of different volumes). Such a process ultimately reaches the point of an infinitely specified, unrepeatable performance event.

We touched on this idea before in Part 1, where we saw how the values of musical variables in relatively concrete electronic music have a greater degree of specification than those of relatively flexible classical music. This process of musical speci-fication also relates to the concentric nature of musical objects within music space as described earlier in Part 2, of course, and is just as applicable to smaller, relatively defined musical objects as it is to music space as a whole. The process can help us imagine how the infinite possibilities of music space (which pertain prior to any specification and are as flexible as its possible to get) are narrowed down to categories of musical objects and then to performances as increasing amounts of increasingly specific information build up. It gives composers a clearer sense of the extents of flexible or (relatively) concrete musical objects and thus a clearer sense of where they stand in relation to the full potential of music space's variability. As we'll see (and somewhat counter-intuitively), the more constrained information composers specify, the more evident the rich possi-bilities of music space become. It'll also lay some groundwork for the discussion of aesthetics (since we perceive and judge music by progressively gathering information about it) and new music in Part 3.

A progressive specification of musical information represents not just the increasing complexity of musical objects themselves, but also a musical system's capacity to constitute those musical objects (which amounts to the same thing). Returning to the list terms that are synonymous with constitution here, it's therefore also an increase in a musical system's capacity to recognise, imagine, create, compose, listen to, describe and define musical objects. As explained earlier in the examples of musical objects as describing systems, a complex musical performance would very poorly constituted by a comparatively simple describing system, just as a colour picture becomes pixellated and its colour palette reduced by a low quality scanner. A comparable system for 'scanning' music, for example, might only specify or recognise two 'shades' (i.e. two possible values) of volume, two 'shades' of pitch and two lengths of duration. It would quantise all the values in the original music to its own limited recognition of values in the process of re-constitution, losing huge amounts of information about the original performance in the process. This system would have a very low 'fidelity' to the original performance and would be very 'lo-fi' indeed. Even if we somehow already knew it, we as listeners wouldn't be able to recognise the original performance.

This progression in music's capacity to constitute musical objects or performances can be illustrated with an analogy of a computer screen acting as an imaging system. Imagine we're trying to see a digital photograph of the planet Earth, fairly large against a backdrop of space, on a square monitor that only consists of a single pixel of any shade with which to display pictures. It has a screen resolution of 1 by 1. All the colour information in the picture has been quantised to that one-pixel system, which would probably be of a dull bluish colour. We certainly wouldn't be able to tell, if we didn't know, that it was originally a picture of the Earth. Now imagine we increase that resolution to four pixels, each of a different shade. Since each quarter of the picture has similar average shades, this wouldn't help much either. If we doubled the number of pixels in the screen's resolution again and again, we would slowly begin to build up a better picture of the Earth, a picture with a greater degree of specific information in it. At around sixty-four pixels (eight pixels along each side of the screen), we might begin to get a sense of a round bluish object against a black backdrop.

As the resolution continued to increase, we'd eventually

realise that the pictures was of a planet, and there would be a certain threshold at which we could recognise it as the Earth. Further on in the process, we would see that the Earth was not just blue, but had green and beige continents and white clouds, all with complex shapes. If our screen were big enough, as the numbers of pixels ran into the millions and billions we'd begin to discern fields, settlements, roads, vehicles and people (by which point the screen would have to be about as big as the Earth itself for our eyes to see them without zooming in). We would be seeing earth in 'hi-fi': high fidelity, or 'high definition' as it's more commonly known. Or we could imagine this process not as one of quantising visual information into discrete pixels, but as a continuous process of receiving more and more accurate information about areas of the picture. In this case, rather than a grid of squares, the Earth would slowly emerge in more detail from a vague, fuzzy blur, just as a telescope comes into focus.

Now imagine that the screen is a creating system analogous to musical composition, constituting pictures anew rather than reconstituting an original picture as before. The effect is the same as if we don't know beforehand that the screen would come to depict Earth. We'd think it could come to depict anything at all, and this is just like music space, with its infinite possibilities pertaining prior to any specific constraining of variables. At first, seeing the single blue pixel, we would know that whatever was on the screen could be put in the broad category of 'blue things'. Later on in the process of specification, having discerned the backdrop of space, we'd surmise that the object was in the subcategory of 'blue astronomical objects' and then 'blue planets'. At this point, the picture could turn out to be of Earth, Uranus, Neptune or any other blue planets we might know. As we began to make out lots of white clouds on the planet, it would enter the subcategory of 'blue Earth-like planets'. If we knew it were impossible or very unlikely that the planet was outside our solar system, we would then know that it was certain (or very likely) to actually be Earth.

If we knew the picture was of Earth, then we'd get a sense of which era we're seeing Earth in once we begin to see continents. If the continents weren't in the position they are today, then it could be a picture of Earth in some previous geological age, such as the Jurassic Period. Again however, we may know that it if it were a photograph, it would be impossible or unlikely that it was taken before the late nineteen-sixties, when humanity became capable of taking such photographs. At this point we know we have a photograph of Earth somewhere between the late nineteen-sixties and the present day. As the resolution of the image increased still further, we'd begin to see features of settlements that could tell us more information about the date the photograph was taken, by looking at whether large buildings or landmarks were present or not. As we begin to see people, and if we had some way of knowing precise details about the position of those people in time, we'd be able to specify the time the picture was taken down to the second. So from a blue blur – which could have turned out to be anything at all that was blue – we've honed in on a much more specific object: the planet Earth, at a very precise time in its existence. The range of things that the picture *could have become* narrowed as the values of the system became more and more specified (more constrained), the image became more and more complex, and the information we had to hand, the information constituted in the picture, increased.

Whether by using ever finer discrete objects like pixels or an approach that creates a continuously clearer impression, this process of 'focusing in' or 'honing in' to constitute ever more specific musical objects, which equates to an ever narrower defined range of performance events, is the same as the process of honing in on specific musical objects through a series of concentric subspaces described earlier. That honing, that process of progressive specification, can be brought about in two ways. The first is by relatively constraining the ranges of the values: a pitch between 200Hz and 300Hz is less specific than a pitch between 240Hz and 260Hz because the former has a range of 100Hz and the latter has a range of 20Hz. The second way is by adding a new constrained variable that hadn't been counted as part of the musical object before: a musical object between 200Hz and 300Hz is less specific than a musical object between 200Hz and 300Hz that *also* has, say, a volume of between 10dB and 20dB. The former could have actualised with any volume at all, as volume wasn't specified in its identity as a musical object.

By specifying both narrower ranges and ranges on new variables, this process progressed forwards along a continuum going from more flexible music to more concrete music and finally to a single point of theoretically infinite specificity. We could also say that this progression was one moving from more basic, relatively *undifferentiated* forms to more complex, relatively *differentiated* forms. Just as a picture of earth with continents and clouds is more specific and differentiated than a vague bluish circle (which could have turned out to be any round blue object), so the jazz music of Miles Davis is a more specific subcategory than the vague category of 'jazz' itself. Jazz is a fuzzier, more statistical musical object, and a much more flexible and undifferentiated musical object too. A far more specified and 'more concrete' musical object would be Miles Davis's performance of February 12th 1964 at the Philharmonic Hall of Lincoln Center, New York. If this musical object 'jazz' were less flexible and more defined, it would begin to lose its ability to constitute a range of performances, and would narrow its range to a subset of jazz. This process of progressive specification ultimately leads to an infinitely concrete and utterly unrepeatable performance event, or one at least as specified as the entire state of universe itself and everything in it can be specified.

Degrees of Freedom

So in a fundamental sense, these two methods of specification –

firstly, specifying narrower ranges and secondly, adding new constrained variables – amount to the same process, that of progressively constituting musical information. Both equally play a part in constraining or specifying the possibilities of music space by assigning ever narrower ranges of possible values on music, whatever variables we use to express those values. To borrow a technical term from science, engineering and statistics, both methods increase the overall *degree of freedom*, which can be expressed as a relative quantity of independent, functionally discrete *degrees of freedom*. Despite their name (the reason for which will shortly become apparent), these degrees of freedom impose narrower ranges on musical variability and can be thought of as independent units each giving us a piece of specifying information about a musical object. As such they combine variables and values into the same thing: a measure of capacity for relative informational complexity, regardless of whether that information has already been assigned (as in a describing system) or not (as in a composing system).

The effect of degrees of freedom can be imagined in two ways, depending on to what extent they either contain or 'bear' specific, assigned information that increases our knowledge about a musical object (as in a describing system) or create a space for a range of possible specifications of information but where information hasn't already been assigned (as in a creating system). When describing a musical object, the higher the number of degrees of freedom we can observe, the narrower the ranges and constraints on what we can know are, and the more specific the information we know about the musical object becomes. On the other hand, when composing musical objects, higher degrees of freedom offer greater opportunities for the specification of musical information. But remember that earlier we brought together describing and composing as the same process, one of 'constituting' musical objects. This allows us to think of musical information in the abstract, without having to separate the gathering of information from a context of open creative possibility. The process of progressive specification, then, is a process in which the number of degrees of freedom that constitute musical objects (and which musical objects can themselves constitute) increases, thus constituting more detailed information about music, and allowing more complex musical forms. To put it more technically, the progressive specification of music space is a *net increase in the number of information-bearing degrees of freedom that constitute it*.[31]

As discussed earlier, there are many ways of constituting the dimensionality of a musical object, but degrees of freedom are the independent constrained variables that any musical object can be boiled down to based on their capacity to convey independent pieces of specific information about a musical object. The more degrees of freedom a musical system (composing or describing) has, the more specified and detailed the musical objects it constitutes. For example, think of a work of concrete music, existing as a file on a computer. There are lots of ways we as human listeners might constitute this musical work as a structure of variables, each reflecting our own needs, capacities and habits. These might include types of timbres used, textures, changes in volume used throughout or at a particular point, the number of times a melody recurs, how harmonies are used, and so on. In the same way, a musical work can be divided into musical objects such as timbres and chords in a large number of different ways.

But to the computer all these variables are boiled down to information-bearing degrees of freedom in the form of binary variables, or 'bits', arranged in a long sequence, the values of which are expressed as either 1 or 0. For the computer's sound-playing software, which is not programmed to concern itself with such musical objects as timbres, melodies, harmonies and textures, each one of these bits is a musical variable giving it useful information on what to play – each bit constitutes one degree of freedom. In this way, the number of musical variables describing the musical objects on a modern mp3 player (i.e. its files) can easily run into the tens of millions. Each bit is a musical object, and any combination of any number of those bits is also conceivably a musical object that that system can constitute. Of course, human composers would hardly be willing or able to produce music by reducing all the variables to binary code, written from scratch, even if its musical possibilities as a medium are virtually infinite.

So confusingly, given their name, a higher number of information-bearing degrees of freedom entails a greater degree of specifying constraints on the form music takes, but for composers they can also be thought of as encouraging a greater freedom *to be* specific. Degrees of freedom only appear to constrain musical variability in describing systems, where variables' values (and the information contained therein) were already specified anyway. In a creating system, however, they represent greater possibilities to differ. For example, a binary musical variable is a degree of freedom that only offers a choice between two states. It could offer two pitches, two volumes, two textures, or even two melodies or two musical works. But as a musical object it's a system that can only differ in one way – it offers an either/or choice between a value of 0 and a value of 1, and that isn't a lot of freedom at all. In this case there is only one degree of freedom. As with the imaging screen, the more bits there are, the more degrees of freedom there are, and the more richly specific the music can be in its details. Tens of millions of information-bearing bits creates a very complex and specific musical object, and tens of millions of bits that have not yet been assigned values offer huge possibilities for musical variability in composition (think of how many different musical performances could be constituted using a few megabytes of information stored on, say, a computer hard drive). Note how these two cases become the same: both represent the same degree of informational complexity, the same degree of freedom, the same quantity of independent degrees of freedom. Imagining those values as if they were as yet unassigned reminds us that the work is just one out of a wide range of possibilities to pertain at the same extent of informational complexity. We come to see the pre-described, pre-assigned object against a background or matrix of similarly constitutable objects. This matrix of imagination is defined by a structure of degrees of freedom, and it is expanded further by both widening the constraints on variables and adding new constrained variables. Both of these techniques increase the degree(s) of freedom in the system and thus build the creative imagination of music space.

A binary variable only offers a choice between two discrete, differentiated options and as such is the simplest kind of variable any music can be reduced to. Degrees of freedom don't always represent binary choices, however. Cage's sound space system had five constrained continuous variables, and thus five degrees of freedom, because there were five pieces of information his system constituted (i.e. created to be known) about sounds: frequency, amplitude, timbre, duration, and morphology, all constrained by the limits of human perception. Each one of those pieces of information represents a much richer potential for musical variability than a computer bit does, of course, but this doesn't alter the fact that as a system Cage's sound space has five degrees of freedom. A musical object could have millions of degrees of freedom as far as a computer system is concerned, but Cage's system constitutes musical objects with just five. This, of course, is the difference between digital and analogue systems. A binary variable is a discrete variable, and a few megabytes of information represents a discrete, finite space composed of bits, just like a computer screen is composed of a finite number of pixels. Tape machines are analogue because they don't express information discretely, as bits, but rather as comparatively smooth patterns of magnetised compounds. Thus the variables in Cage's sound space were continuous, and so the space was a continuous space of infinite possibilities. Prior to the specification of any discrete variables, music space is a continuous space, too.

Unlike Cage's sound space though, music space doesn't have a fixed number of degrees of freedom – or rather, it can be thought of as having (the capacity for) an infinite number of differentiated degrees of freedom. The progressive specification of music space sees it in terms of a net increase in descriptive or compositional degrees of freedom. It starts with one degree of freedom, then two, then three and so on until there are as many degrees of freedom as the universe or the imagination can constitute. This process can be visualised as a tree that branches off into more differentiated forms, with one formal possibility becoming two and so on – much like the 'tree of life' in biology, where one species branches off into two separate species, which in turn become three or four separate species and so on. We can imagine the differentiation of musical objects in a similar way to how evolution proceeds from relatively simple forms like basic multicellular life develop into many diverse kingdoms of complex biological variety – octopi, hedgehogs, grasshoppers, giant redwoods, dinosaurs, lobsters, camels, fungi, whales, flamingos, orchids, manta rays, chameleons, cabbages and humans. Like the imagining system's screen that came to depict the Earth in all its richness, life progressively differentiates into specific complex forms as categories become more specific: kingdom (e.g. animalia, animals) becomes phylum (e.g. chordata, animals with something like a spine), phylum becomes class (e.g. mammalia, mammals), then order (e.g. primates), family (e.g. hominidae, great apes), genus (e.g. *homo*, awhich includes a number of species including Neanderthals), species (e.g. *homo sapiens*, modern humans) and finally a particular individual. This process could be thought of as the progressive specification of 'life space', and is analogous to the same process in the imagining and composition of music. We can imagine, for example, new and different life forms and categories of life forms arising from the same life space, lying 'in between' or 'beyond' those that already exist or have existed (as in works of speculative biology, where the evolution of alternative life forms, terrestrial or extraterrestrial, is imagined), and we can do the same for music.

Music can display a comparable diversity, but unlike that of biological evolution its tree of diversity isn't fixed and hierarchical. There is no one 'root' to the tree of musical specification, no one variable that is always assigned or determined first in the specification process, because it can conceivably start with any constrained variable at all and progress in its specification through further degrees of freedom in any way and any order. Rather than 'roots', there are simply areas with fewer degrees of freedom, which may represent any constrained variables at all, even those with values that are complex 'higher' structures like texture or harmony. Besides which, very different musical objects can combine in ways that species can't. A tree of progressive musical diversity is more like a highly multidimensional thicket that can be entered and exited in any place, and through which any path, however irregular, can be traced. This progressive path-making through the variability of music space is, of course, exactly the activity of composing and listening to music.

As the number of degrees of freedom increases, and the detail of compositional control increases, so flexible musical objects become more concrete. Eventually, the number of degrees of freedom reaches some limit, which could be that of the number of degrees of freedom in a describing system such as a computer or in the ultimate describing system, the universe itself. With concrete musical objects no further degrees of compositional freedom are held to pertain – they are single points, constituted by systems, with no degrees of freedom with which to differ (i.e. reach a still more specific subset) at the point of performance. In flexible music we admit that there are still some 'compositional' or creative degrees of freedom left over to bear more specific information at the point of performance. Thus the idea of a progressive specification of musical objects tells us that there's a point at which the composers' degrees of freedom end and where other degrees of freedom pertain. We can theoretically sketch a line halfway along the progressive specification that shows the 'cut-off point' where the composers' degrees of freedom end and those that are even more specific start, say, at the point of the performers. This gives us all the more reason not to ultimately divide music space's information-potential into separate activities of 'creating' and 'describing', but a general process of constituting music that can then be differentiated into the domains of various agencies (composer, performer, listener etc.), with respect to their control over information.

For example, many constrained variables in a musical score have their values assigned by composers, but in a performance of that musical work many other degrees of freedom specify that particular performance *beyond the* domain of the composers' control over values. Those degrees of freedom that come after the composers are the domain of the performers and other participants, but are ultimately the domain of the universe itself (and we can't step into the same universe twice: like the river, its degrees of freedom are constantly changing their values). Composers, then, are only partially responsible for their music's specific attributes – the real musician is the universe itself. But composers can choose to place themselves and their music at any point along the progressive specification of music, writing basic, more flexible music, or highly specified, more concrete music. This latter category might include non-sonic variables, because when they are assigned values they make performance events even more specific.

When composers are far down the progressive specification and assign information to a larger number of degrees of freedom, this decreases the amount of certainty that a describing system has about what that music might be in its specifics before it is heard. On the other hand, when 'describers' (describing systems, listeners, musical analysts) have a larger number of information-bearing degrees of freedom concerning a musical object, the composers of that musical object have less freedom to specify values themselves. Theoretically, if the composers' freedom is infinite, corresponding to the pure, unconstrained variability of music space itself, then the amount of prior, constraining information a describer has is zero. If the describers have all the specific information about a musical object, meaning that all its degrees of freedom bear specific information and the musical object is concrete, then it is the composers (and by extension the performers and participants) who have zero freedom. So composers and describers meet each other at some point midway along the progressive specification of music, in a tug-of-war over prior compositional freedoms and prior descriptive certainty. We can avoid imposing this dichotomy and the assumptions inherent in it by considering musical information as purely 'constituted' by degrees of freedom.

Extrapolating a Music Space from Performance Events

So to sum up: the quantity of degrees of freedom in a system gives the extent of its informational complexity, whether we think of them as having values assigned or not. Now it would be easy to assume that a single degree of freedom represents a basic musical characteristic such as pitch or timbre, or specific pitches or timbres, but this is not necessarily the case. Just as single constrained variables can build up into complex forms like textures, a degree of freedom can represent any musical object, however complex we might consider it to be. We can progressively specify music space and discover its possibilities using entire musical performances as single degrees of freedom, with each work becoming a data point that adds informational complexity to a *sample* of music space. In this way we can extrapolate a sense of the breadth of music space's variability or a subspace thereof. This is the same progressive specification as that described earlier – an increase in complexity through increasing degrees of freedom – but it proceeds from entire musical performances rather than constrained variables of a crude kind (for example those two 'shades' of pitch or volume). This better reflects our musical experience, of course, since we hear actual, fully-fledged and complex musical performances during our lives rather than a series of more and more information-rich forms. As these performances increase in number they progressively specify, or 'open up', music space(s) within our imaginations.

Say we were trying to build up a picture of the specific kinds of variability that jazz music entails as a musical object between individual musical performances, and had a sample of five jazz recordings (such the five tracks on *My Funny Valentine*, the record made from recordings of Miles Davis performing live at the Lincoln Center) to do that with. In this case our 'sample of jazz' would have four degrees of freedom. There are four rather than five degrees of freedom because if we just had one recording, there would be no room for the system to differ, but if we had two there'd be one way for it to differ, which would make it a binary variable – so we subtract one from the total number of samples to find the number of degrees of freedom. These five jazz recordings would themselves constitute a musical object: a system with four degrees of freedom just as Cage's sound space constituted one with five. But instead of existing within dimensions of frequency, volume, duration and so on, the music that the 'jazz sample' system constituted would move between these five sampled performances, in a space that could be thought of as being *opened up* by them, with each successive sampled performance amounting to a single constrained dimensional variable.[32] Add a new jazz recording to the system and a further degree of freedom is added, and more space is opened up. For someone looking to extrapolate jazz as a musical object from the information given by the sampled performances, this means they have further information on what jazz might really be. (The space is even more opened up to what jazz might really be in its entirety if we add a jazz recording to the system that differs quite considerably from *My Funny Valentine*, a recording of Dixieland jazz or free jazz, for example.) For someone looking to compose music using that system, this means they have more options for musical variability. This all illustrates how a musical object – in this case a constrained structure of variables as complex as a recording of a jazz performance – can be represented as a single constrained variable: a single unit of constrained information, a degree of freedom. Similarly, the huge and detailed difference between two performances can be expressed by a single variable whose values pass between two states.

Imagine jazz recordings were being sampled as performances in just this way by a group of spatially and biologically distant alien beings, who have somehow obtained *My Funny Valentine* as a sole example of the human music that is jazz. With just the one recording, the aliens know nothing about how the music varies from performance to performance. With or without the aid of special equipment, they probably observe pitches and volumes changing over time, of course, but as far as they're concerned, jazz could change in any way at all *between performances* on Earth. As far as the aliens know, the entirety of the jazz tradition could simply amount to the five tracks on *My Funny Valentine* played over and over again, but shifted in their entirety to slightly different speeds, pitches, timbres or orders each time, for example. (They also wouldn't know that the applause after each solo and at the start and end of the tracks indicates a live audience of listeners, and is not considered 'part of the music', nor are the applauders considered to be participating 'musicians'.) The aliens have no way of knowing about the complex rules and variabilities of jazz music as it exists between performances.

Once they have five jazz recordings, however, the aliens know a huge amount more about jazz and the ways in which it varies between performances while remaining within the locus of the same musical object. The more recordings the aliens collect, the more they learn about jazz, though the amount they learn relative to what they already know decreases a little each time on average – after a thousand jazz recordings, their impression of jazz is unlikely to change much even if they acquire a thousand more. The aliens won't know how many recordings it'll take until they 'know' the musical object that we call jazz in some potentially sufficient way – that is, how many degrees of freedom they'll need for a sufficient sample – but jazz doesn't have a finite definition that can be 'known' in this way, or indeed that needs to be known. It only has statistical patterns that apply up to the present day, and when the aliens see little more than these statistical patterns confirmed with each successive recording, they'll know that they're approaching the limit of the information necessary to 'know' jazz, even if they'll never actually reach it. If, on the other hand, the aliens only wanted to know *My Funny Valentine* as a musical object, strictly in its capacity as a structure of musical information, then they've already got all they need.

Now imagine that we're the ones receiving alien music. Again, with only one sample of this music, we'd have no way of knowing how that music varies from performance to performance back on the alien planet, and it could do so in complex, unusual and unexpected ways. We wouldn't know how many more examples we'll need before we've got an adequate impression of the alien music – we wouldn't know how broad the locus of its variability gets, how many millions or billions of degrees of compositional freedom the alien music enjoys. We wouldn't know how much or how little we knew about the whole picture: how far apart our collected examples were across the span of the total 'alien music space', what extent and sort of variation we could deduce in similar examples back on their planet, or how small or subtle the musical variation could be (the aliens might only ever have 'performed music' a handful of times and sent all the recordings, for example). If we hear widely different styles, we may not even know whether they were produced by the same species. We may need millions of performance samples of their music before we've got a good enough impression of the locus of variability in alien music. Actually, unless it was identifiably addressed to listeners like us directly, we may not even know that it was 'music' rather than some form of other communication between the aliens. We'd be wrong to assume it was an example of the same or a similar concept of 'music' that we have – all we'd know is that it was a sign of alien life in the universe.[31]

Of course, this is exactly the problem facing any aliens who may happen to find the Voyager Golden Record. Its twenty-seven musical performances were specially chosen to give a particularly broad and diverse sample, encompassing human music-making in a number of its many varieties. We, back on Earth, already know a great deal about the finer levels of variability in our music, so we can recognise that it comes closer to representing the entire locus of human music's pure variability than most other musical objects, and thus opens up a much larger area of music space. But we also know that it would take a statistical sample of human music with uncountable millions of degrees of freedom for an outsider to begin to appreciate the diverse complexity of musical variability the way we collectively do.

Where Cage's sound space showed what sort of sounds were available in a broad sense, the Voyager Golden Record complements it as a space of possibilities that shows not just what sort of sounds are available, but also something about the complex and deeply differentiated stylistic specifics that can be (and have been) achieved in human music. The Golden Record is to musical diversity what Noah's Ark is to biological diversity. While Cage's sound space gives us the big picture, the Golden Record gives a good impression of how detailed the picture can get.

Music Space and New Music

Here we can sum up what this philosophy of infinite music space means for composers. Its system of infinite musical variability puts all currently existing music into the context of its much wider and unrealised possibilities. Music space is the opened-up continuous phase space upon which all the concrete musical performances that have existed up to this moment can be plotted as single points, arranged in tiny clusters where performances are similar to each other, and spaced widely apart in our imaginations by a distance of as yet unactualised possibilities. As with those aliens slowly coming to appreciate the scope of human music-making by increasing their collection of recorded performances, these plotted points are the data we have received to date in a sample that hints at the scope of musical variability itself. In identifying the small number of loosely defined musical objects we've collected so far, we draw imprecise, multidimensional lines, forming shapes that group together collections of these points as we might do around sets of numbers in a data printout, counting them as single musical objects – the piano, the style called 'jazz', the musical work 'Behind the Mask', for example. Many more clusters of points await this grouping of information that identifies musical objects, especially shapes intersecting more unconventional dimensionalities. But everywhere in music space and even beneath these groupings, there's infinite room for new, multidimensional musical possibilities.

Music space reveals to composers all the gaps and limitations in the conventions of the past and present, and all that hasn't been composed yet, by situating it against a backdrop of alternative possibilities. It's a map of musical possibility, currently sparsely dotted with settlements. The innovations of the twentieth century discovered the outermost extremes of this map, and some composers established well-known outposts there. This frontier phase of discovery culminated in Cage's sound space, which draws a basic perimeter around humanly audible sound, with everything within that realm of sound now accessible for musical composition. The vehicle Cage proposed for traversing this space was magnetic tape, which allowed composers such as Stockhausen and Edgard Varèse to explore spaces far beyond those of the more conventional sounds of their time. But compared to modern technology, tape is so relatively crude and awkward a tool for the composition of concrete music today that it's now often accompanied by an aesthetics of nostalgia or ironic frailty.

Ever since Cage, and especially in the technological milieu of the new millennium, a second phase of innovation has begun: the infinite task of colonising the entirety of music space. The technology to do this has existed since Cage's time, but it's fast becoming a lot more readily available, more nuanced and easier to learn and use. No longer are unconventional sounds the preserve of lone musical astronauts encased in multi-million dollar banks of consoles and miles of electrical wire, with their handfuls of short trips to alien worlds. They are being created and practiced all over the world, every day, by new generations of composers using increasingly accessible technology, in a musical revolution that looks set to advance dramatically over the coming decades. These composers aren't just *experimenting* with these sounds, merely visiting these alien worlds for the sake of formal exploration. They're *living* in these worlds – worlds that for them and their audiences have just as much meaningful detail as any of the traditional musics of the past.

This is the age of *post-experimental music*. After the experiments of the twentieth century, musical innovation must now turn *inward* and explore the uncovered territory of music space in all its complex details. This is not at all the same thing as turning backwards, since musical innovation is multidirectional within and throughout the infinite dimensions of music space. Besides, you can't claim to really know a whole country if you've only flown to five of its outermost corners. Nor would this inwardly innovative music necessarily sound familiar to present-day listeners. This innovation is inspired by the depth and richness of musical diversity as revealed so aptly by the Voyager Golden Record – not by any opportunity to literally adopt those musical objects that already exist on it (which would certainly be the wrong from of colonisation), but by encountering the space hinted at by the array of complex and deeply differentiated styles it reveals and celebrates as being specific parts of a single music space. If every musical object is also an imagining system, then the Golden Record opens up a space, both wide and detailed, for composers' imaginations like few others. This demonstrates what composers should already have known – that the more different kinds of music you know and understand, the easier it is to imagine the possibilities for further kinds of music. But even those performances on it represent a very limited sample of human music-making potential, weighted as it was towards classical music, omitting more experimental forms of classical, jazz, rock and electronic music, and being launched before electronic popular music flourished.

The newly accessible infinity of music space, criss-crossed with the pathways of change represented by each musical variable, can lead composers to new music. Musical variables, both basic and complex, show composers the avenues of musical change they may have forgotten, revealing how worn-out the old paths of musical convention are and providing escape routes from them into new dimensions when new ones are used. Musical objects – a category in which styles, instruments, works and any other more unusual musical tool currently without a name become equivalent and continuous – are the structures that composers invent, adapt and re-use, and that listeners identify, appreciate and cherish. The specification of music space from flexible to concrete forms shows composers the extent to which there may be variables and values (combining to form degrees of freedom) that they haven't specified, or that they may leave to performers or other participants. All this is certainly not to imply that composers should agonise over all the minute effects of all the variables or musical objects they may or not be using, calculate their own degrees of freedom and generally compose music in a systematic or scientific manner as a finely tuned structure of variables. Composition may remain as fluid and intuitive as ever. But all this is at least to make composers as *conscious* as possible of all the avenues they're missing out on and what they can take advantage of – or what they're choosing to ignore.

More than this, however, infinite music space presents composers, and to some extent listeners, with an ethos of musical composition. It is towards the pure, unconstrained variability of music space that composers should aspire and direct themselves, and for which listeners should hunger. In their capacities as individuals or groups of people with a recurring audience, composers must open up as much of music space as they can in just the same way that the Voyager Golden Record does – by constantly switching to new and wildly differentiated variables, styles and musical objects. If they are particularly skilled composers, they'll be able to do this while still retaining, or establishing anew, some degree of aesthetic meaning relatable to themselves and their listeners, walking the tightrope between new and familiar musical languages. In this way, as with the aliens receiving samples of human music-making, a space is opened up in the listeners' imagination. Furthermore, the larger the departure that the new music makes from the previous music, the larger the space of imagination opened up between them, allowing composers to expand the imaginations of those who listen carefully enough. It would not be an exaggeration to say that if music is continuous with life, and not separate, discrete, 'above it' and largely meaningless to it as old, limiting ideologies held it to be, then composers who expand their listener's musical imaginations will be expanding their capability to imagine new forms of art and new forms of life.

In the next part we'll look at the nature of musical listening, considering how we perceive musical objects according to our own prior interests, biases and assumptions. This will lead us to replace musical objects with corresponding *images of music*. We'll see how this gives rise to judgements of value and originality regarding both individual musical performances and music as a whole. This will lead us to a definition of new music along with an understanding of how composers might go about creating it effectively and how listeners might perceive it adequately.

Part 3: Aesthetics and Music Space

Having discovered the infinite resources of music space and how composers might makes use of them, this part begins with what might at first appear to be a severe setback: the vast majority of music space is practically useless to human listeners.

Not every possible permutation of sound will have an equal appeal to humans, and in fact most of these permutations will have little lasting appeal for us at all. We can learn see this by generating sound randomly. Imagine, for example, a composing programme on a modern computer, where all musical variables are boiled down to their finest, densest, most detailed possible structure of information, that of the degrees of freedom in binary code. The number of degrees of freedom making up a musical object can vary, of course, but let's say each of this programme's compositions will be a certain number of bits long, and that each of these bits was understood by a computer as a musical variable expressing amplitudes in time to which the composing programme could assign a value of either 0 or 1. As a composing system, this computer can thus constitute a truly enormous number of different musical performances. But if the programme freely randomised those bits, then well over 99.9% of the times the programme was run, the results – even though they'd all be wildly differentiated from each other – would merely appear to human listeners as what is called 'white noise'.

White noise is the sound an untuned analogue radio or television makes, and is similar to the sound of a large waterfall up close or a constant vocalised 'sh' sound. It's not an inherently unattractive noise – white noise and sounds like it have been used to great effect in many musical objects and performances. Even a musical work that does little more than slowly filter the frequencies of white noise over time can make for a very interesting listening experience comparable to viewing a twentieth-century abstract colour field painting. We might even be able to say that such a work had an emotional as well as a purely formal appeal. People can listen to white noise for long stretches of time and quite rightly appreciate it. But only the most infinitely adventurous (or stoical) human listener would be content to listen to nothing other than unadorned white noise, seeing all their musical needs forever met by that random composition machine.

Why is this the case? Surely this randomised binary code is the freest and most detailed music there can possibly be? If the goal of composers is to open up the imaginative freedom of music space and actualise as much of it as possible, then doesn't randomised white noise – which changes its entire structure thousands of times every second and in which anything is possible – represent this *par excellence*? Perhaps we should all just listen to white noise forever more, if it's the richest music there is.

We can't do this, of course. With its ability to listen to or 'sample' individual sounds thousands of times a second, a computer may be able to 'appreciate' the rich flow of information in white noise, but a human brain can't constitute the same number of information-bearing degrees of freedom a computer can at that speed. So if we were listening to all of music space equally, then practically all we would ever hear would be white noise. The situation is similar to the famous thought experiment in which a very large number of monkeys type on a very large number of typewriters for a very long time. With a large enough number of monkeys and a large enough length of time, eventually the monkeys will type the complete works of Shakespeare without a single mistake. This would be very unlikely to happen in the lifetime of an impatient human onlooker, and then there would be all those millions of times in which the monkeys nearly got there but spelled a single word wrongly. Even if the keys the monkeys had in front of them were all the words Shakespeare had used, readymade, it would still take an eternity to put them in the right order, or to write anything that makes sense at all. If all we ever wanted from literature were letters or words in any order at all, there'd be no need for human authors – a monkey could do it.

Digital white noise is the sound of millions of electronic monkeys, each on typewriters with only two keys. It's *possible* of course, that the randomising computer would eventually output Miles Davis's *My Funny Valentine*. But the difference here is that we don't even possess the perceptive faculties to tell what's going on within the sound typically generated by the randomisation, whereas with the Shakespeare example we could at least perceive the letters and nonsense words that the monkeys type. All we hear in white noise is an apparently homogenous blur, because the information within the noise is so finely-grained. Even if we created a slightly more advanced composing machine in which rhythms could be created, or frequencies lasted for a perceptible length of time, or there were a finite number of timbres to choose from, the machine's output would very rarely achieve the level of satisfaction we get when listening to our favourite music over and over again. Besides which, music is of course more than just the sound it makes, and there's very often something appealing about listening to music as being the product of a human being or a particular human being. For example, if a computer could randomise a typical Miles Davis performance perfectly I may enjoy the sound, but a part of me would feel duped and the experience would be diminished – this would be a clear example of non-sonic appeal in music. And wouldn't there be some sounds that those composing machines couldn't do that we may like to hear in music? Noise music, for example, often gets quite close to the qualities of white noise but has a dedicated and growing audience nevertheless.

We have to admit, then, that there are some musical objects more suited to the specific needs and listening capabilities of human listeners than others. To take this into consideration, music space can be presented as *human music space*, a subspace whose contents are loosely organised according to their likely suitability for extended human listening. These human preferences and discriminations can be imagined as overlaid or projected onto music space – human interest 'maps' human music space onto music space. All the musical objects we think of as white noise and everything else in music space would be contained within this human music space, but it would be presented as less likely to satisfy extended human listening than other musical objects and would accordingly have less significance within human music space. The characteristics and quantities that structure human music space can't be precisely given, of course. They'll vary between listeners and groups of listeners, over time and throughout history, not to mention the ways in which listening to one musical performance may affect the way listeners then listen to a subsequent performance. So we can only talk about the properties of human music space in the vaguest sense. It tells us, for example, that much of music space (that is, all the different permutations the random binary code composing machine could constitute, which are predominantly white noise) effectively appears to be 'the same' musical object to human listeners. It can't practically be differentiated according to the same number of degrees of freedom a computer observes – it doesn't have an appeal for human listeners equivalent to the amount of music space it takes up. Similarly, human music space allows for a human's inability to differentiate miniscule differences in pitch, volume, timbre, duration or any other variable whose virtually infinitesimally altered values we might believe to have remained 'the same'. There may be an infinite number of possible pitches in an octave as measured continuously in hertz, but a human can typically only recognise a division of the octave into a few dozen different discrete pitches at most.

Here we must be very careful. Because music space can be structured this way – effectively prioritising its contents according to the propensities of human listeners – it would be very easy to slip into overly conservative or culturally contingent notions about which musical characteristics are preferable to others. What's more, we must be especially careful not to unwittingly accept such notions disguised by a propaganda of pseudo-biological pragmatism or evolutionary-psychological 'human reality' and finitude. Human music space is just as large as music space and just as infinite, the only difference is that there's a very vague and minimal topography of human preference overlaid onto it. We don't yet know the full extent of the human musical imagination and what it could now or one day come to appreciate. History has seen its capacity expand, and there's no reason to assume that during the twentieth century it reached its apex, much less that we should renege on the convention-shattering musical adventures of the last century.[34] Human music space represents nothing more than the barest human musical capacity and discrimination, and doesn't take in cultural tastes. It doesn't imply, along the traditional conservative lines, that human music ought to be melodic, harmonic, adopt the notes and practices of the Western or Western classical system, be complex, be simple, be played by those taken to be accomplished performers, be listened to passively or even that it should 'make sense' to a listener (whatever that might be taken to mean).

Such restrictive ideas may seem like common sense, but they are not absolute laws of human musical appreciation. A short examination of the breadth and diversity of human musical cultures throughout history and the world – much of which is collected on the Voyager Golden Record – will quickly invalidate those opinions. Nor does human music space imply that composers ought to head straight for the provinces of human music space that they believe are most likely to appeal to human listeners. In doing this they may not be stoking the imaginations of their listeners very much at all, so composers should aim for the reverse and deliberately head away from the well-trodden paths, or else achieve a careful balance between familiar and unfamiliar appeals, as we'll see later on.

Nevertheless, if composers are to have any effect on their human listeners at all, then human music space is a necessary concern. To reject this minimal imposition of human interest onto musical variability as too much of a compromise would be to assume that we'd have no problem listening to all of music space equally and hearing white noise over 99.9% of the time we press 'play'. Though we're doing so in the most restrained way possible – cautiously conscious of how we must never underestimate the potential diversity of the human musical imagination – by considering which musical objects are more preferential for listening and how, why and when this is the case, we have entered the domain of *aesthetics*: the study of how appealing or unappealing attributes and other appreciable qualities are perceived in art or life in general.

We'll see that if music is a complex system of variables, then the aesthetics of music operates through *that very same system of variables*. The composition of music and the aesthetics of music – that is, the way we listen to music – are not separate concerns, but one and the same process. The activities of composing and listening both 'constitute' musical information: they both 'recognise', 'imagine', '(re)create', 'define', 'specify' and 'describe' its attributes. The only difference is that the listeners' freedom to constitute this musical information is to some extent constrained by the musical information they're presented with, much of which has already been partly specified by the composers. This means that music is not just a certain something that we listen to, it's also an aesthetics of all sound and all life: it's actively constructed by the listener through a particular *way of listening*. Music is in the ear of the beholder, so to speak.

Active, Interested Listening

We don't normally consider everything we listen to or everything in our lives to be music, although Cage taught us that we can do and we can accordingly consider music to be continuous with life. When we happen to hear birdsong, for example, we're not formally 'listening to music' in the traditional way, but we can come to have an aesthetic appreciation of the sound it makes that's comparable to that of music. We might even listen with more interest and attention than we sometimes do to what is more conventionally called music. Music is aesthetically derived from what we hear or experience, a certain active aesthetic 'understanding' of the environmental information available to us. This word 'understanding' shouldn't be taken to imply that there's an absolute, 'correct' way to constitute music's attributes (i.e. musical information) as a listener. And again, there's no simple, absolute way to separate a specifically 'musical' under-standing from any other aesthetic understanding or even any other kind of understanding reached during the course of our lives at all. We don't magically cross some border into 'music' when listening to and understanding the features of our environment, with music being separate from all other kinds of perception. Music is simply the name certain cultures give to a slightly more poetical or artistic understanding of sound-making activities. This reflects how music isn't absolutely distin-guishable from the activities of life, and by extension how life is aesthetics and how music itself is aesthetics. Music is living.

So if we construct music out of what we listen to, then we're effectively composing music out of what we hear. Is this really the case? In a manner of speaking yes, although this 'composing' is only a way of actively assembling in the mind some specific information suggested to the listener during the act of listening. This act of assembly is constrained by the limited capacity of the specific information offered in the music. When we listen to the output of the randomised binary code composing machine (assuming that it didn't fortuitously play some more traditional music), the information we receive as human beings isn't a specific string of ones and zeros, but a basic set of attributes: no particular pitch or frequency, just an apparently homogenous duration of sound. Like the describing system that rendered the Earth as an indistinct blue blur, the human brain (re)constitutes white noise as a constant undifferentiated drone because the resolution of its 'pixels' (the information-bearing degrees of freedom) aren't finely grained enough to constitute anything else. The brain can't 'sample' the white noise at a fast enough rate. In unaided human music space all the different permutations of white noise are effectively constituted as *the same, undifferentiated musical object*, even if the computer, with its different, particular patterns of ones and zeros, would know otherwise.

But if musical aesthetics is the prioritising of certain musical objects over others, what is this prioritisation and how does it work? On top of our physical inability to constitute certain types of musical information, we discriminate between certain types of musical information when listening, depending on our past experiences and certain *interests* related to them, and how they develop during listening. When we listen to music, we don't gather and process every single piece of information that we physically can. Consciously or (more usually) unconsciously, some variables and values are for various reasons more important to us than others, or become more important during listening. For example, when listening to a simple musical work made up of discrete notes, we don't normally purposely care about the total number of notes there are in the entire work as a musical variable (unless we happen to have a specific interest in that number). As relatively casual listeners we're more likely to care about how many notes are in particular sub-melodies and sub-phrases, and moreover what their pitch relationships are, how long they last and so on. We may not be interested in the volume unless it's too loud or soft for us, or changes dramatically. We may not even find it necessary to be particularly conscious of all the different timbres that are used. Or alternatively, we may have specific reason to differentiate the volume and timbre information. When we listen to music, (re)constituting it in our minds, we only collect and constitute musical information *according to the needs and interests that we've developed prior to listening or develop during listening*, whatever they might be.

We listen to music with different levels of interest in which variables and values we'll constitute. This interest may be an intensely attentive concentration that differentiates a large amount of musical information and constructs a finely detailed picture of the music's attributes to the best of our abilities (remember, we're talking of 'interested in' more as in 'having in a stake in' than its narrower meaning 'intrigued by' or 'entertained by'). Or it may be a lesser interest, in which we only really constitute a small amount of information about the music's attributes, for example concluding that the music's style is 'jazz' or 'jazz-like', that it's 'loud', that it's played on trumpets. But listening to music is never a passive experience witnessed from an absolute, pure and *disinterested* viewpoint, an idea that has become increasingly influential in the last two centuries. We don't sit in receptive contemplation while the complete musical score is faxed to some office in our brains and slowly printed out in time to the music as if we were having some specific orders communicated directly to us. To varying extents both consciously and unconsciously, we actively assemble, construct and indeed '(re)compose' the music's attributes as a structure of musical information consisting of variables and values as we listen, according to our needs and interests.

So how do these discriminatory needs and interests arise? They're the result of our being living, learning creatures in a living world with a wealth of prior experience and concerns that stretch beyond any culturally imposed borders that might surround what we term musical activity. We don't hang our worldly social, personal and other needs and interests at the door when we evaluate and (re)constitute music, and though they can have a greater or lesser effect in different circumstances they are right at the heart of how and why we listen to music. Even if we try our hardest to listen attentively and objectively, music isn't separate from its outside world but often an activity within it and of great significance to it. We listen to music – indeed, we 'music' – by means of its capacity to meet these needs.

The psychologist James Gibson introduced the term *affordance* to describe the capacity of objects in our environment to meet the interests we have as creatures in the world:

When the constant properties of constant objects are perceived (the shape, size, colour, texture, composition, motion, animation and position relative to other objects), the observer can go on to detect their *affordances*... [By this] I mean simply what things furnish, for good or ill. What they *afford* the observer, after all, depends on their properties. The simplest affordance, as food, for example, or as a predatory enemy, may well be detected without learning by the young of some animals, but in general learning is all-important for this kind of perception. The child learns what things are manipulable, and how they can be manipulated, what is hurtful, what things are edible, what things can be put together with other things or put inside other things – and so on without limit. He also learns what objects can be used as the means to obtain a goal, or to make other desirable objects, or to make people do what he wants them to do. In short, the human observer learns to detect what have been called the values or meanings of things, perceiving their distinctive features, putting them into categories and subcategories, noticing their similarities and differences and even studying them for their own sakes, apart from learning what to do about them. All this discrimination, wonderful to say, has to be based entirely on the education of his attention to the subtleties of invariant stimulus information.[35]

Note that this description of a learning child can equally resemble the activities of both listening to *and* composing music, and that affordance depends on the attributes of objects, that is, the values of variables). Later in his work, Gibson emphasised that affordance is more than the static observation of usage via the senses of a creature that learns and adapts, but that it also 'implies the complementarity of the animal and the environment'.[36] Affordance is a two-way process, reliant on and achieved through the capacities of both a creature (given by a combination of its experience and its needs) and an object (given by its attributes). In his book *Ways of Listening*, the musicologist Eric Clarke applied this term to music's capacity for meaning, explaining the concept as 'the product both of objective properties and the capacities and needs of the organism that encounters them',[37] and as 'the reciprocity between listeners' capacities and environmental opportunities'.[38] He points out the relativity and flexibility of affordances:

> To a person, a wooden chair affords sitting, while to a termite, it affords eating. Equally, the same chair affords self-defence to a person under attack – an illustration of the way in which an organism can notice different affordances according to its own changing needs. The relationship is neither a case of organisms imposing their needs on an indifferent environment, nor a fixed environment determining possibilities: to a person, a chair can afford sitting and self-defence, but simply cannot afford eating because of the relationship between the capabilities of the human digestive system and the properties of wood. Note that the principle of affordance does not imply that perception will always be obvious and unambiguous, since objects and events can give rise to more than one perceptual experience.[39]

Clarke notes that for Gibson, 'affordances are primarily understood as the *action* consequences of encountering perceptual information in the world', and that along the same lines 'music affords dancing, worship, co-ordinated working, persuasion, emotional catharsis, marching, foot-tapping, and a myriad of other activities of a perfectly tangible kind.' However,

> In certain musical traditions (and the concert music of the West is an obvious example) listening to music has become somewhat divorced from overt action – has become apparently autonomous... A concentration on common or garden objects might lead to the erroneous conclusion that affordances are a simple matter of physical properties and perceptual capacities. But even the most cursory consideration of some more socially embedded objects demonstrates the importance of the social component. A violin, for example, affords burning, but social factors ensure that this is a rather remote affordance.[40]

Whether they're tangible or auditory, then, musical objects *afford* certain uses and meanings depending on our interests – on what we can do with them – and our ability to detect their attributes as musical information. Affordance can be a simple matter: if we simply want to dance then music with strong, regular rhythm has that capacity and meets that need.[41] If we're listening to music in an attentive, complex, and more information-rich way rather than simply deciding what we can get up and do about it, affordance still applies in a similar fashion to how a poem or a novel might afford different 'interpretations' or 'readings' for different people. Affordance isn't just the domain of listeners, either, and can be an important part of composition, with musical objects having affordances that develop for composers as they compose. Music may afford both positive and negative responses too, depending on previously learned associations with certain attributes.

Affordance is also partly dependent on our expectations of music. Having learned something about what is predictable in music we might expect a certain something to recur in performance, and require to some extent that the appropriate musical objects will afford it. But at the same time musical objects can also create and modify those expectations, because affordance is 'dialectical or mutual', a dynamic process incorporating learning.[42] We may not be explicitly aware of precisely what it was we required from a musical object, but it can both meet and develop these requirements, and affect the affordance we derive from other relevant musical objects. As Gibson described it, affordance is an informed, interested and dynamic access to and discrimination of information, often dependent on learning. As a concept it aptly expresses the relativism of aesthetic responses, brings aesthetics back into our wider lives and suggests a way in which particular meanings in art and life become possible. It accords with the idea of music as a system of variables because affordance is a process mediated by the specific attributes of objects – that is, the values of variables.

Again, it would be easy for this concept of affordance to be taken as implying that musical aesthetics is nothing more than an animal's reaction to its environment. The concept of affordance might describe aesthetic responses, but it is not itself to be taken as an ethics of listening, a guide to how listening 'should' be done. While an animal does draw on affordances, it would be wrong to take the concept of affordance as revealing aesthetics to be little more than a biological or social imperative for recently evolved cavemen, bearing clubs that afford killing dinner and singing songs that afford social consolidation in the tribe. The conclusion here would be that loud or discordant noises have the same affordances today that they did for cavemen – danger – so they're unsuitable, unjustified, unsurpassable and aesthetically void for modern humans. Similarly, music that appears disordered or that exceeds whatever degree of comprehension we might deem sufficient is not universally unsuited to human listening. Affordances constantly change with circumstances and can equally be the product of civilised culture, which like humanity is still evolving. More to the point, humans can have a significant degree of control over the process of affordance. We aren't doomed to our animal imperatives and reactions to stimuli, but can learn to see and use these stimuli in a number of complex and informative ways, as Gibson explained. We have learned to (and we continue to) listen to music with an open mind – but this mustn't trick us into believing that musical listening is generally autonomous and disinterested. Our affordance of music can draw on needs, interests and associations we might not be fully aware of, and lead us to make claims for aesthetic value or lack thereof that are not as objective, autonomous and disinterested as we might believe them to be.

Images of Music

By means of the two-way process of affordance, then, aesthetic responses discriminate between all the potential pieces of information musical objects can offer a listener and come to constitute a particular structure or subset of features, effectively presented to them as a structure of constrained variables. This process will only constitute some variables, values and musical objects while the rest will be discounted, effectively undetected, or allotted a more peripheral status. In Part 1 this process was called 'taking variables into account in a musical context' and in Part 2 it was called 'constituting a musical object'. It doesn't just happen during listening itself but *between listenings*, and affects our assumptions, opinions and expectations about what we think make up certain musical objects away from actual musical performances. In this way, affordance generates a certain representation or ideal of a musical object we could call an *image of music*.

Not to be confused with an actual pictorial representation of music, this word 'image' – related, of course, to the word 'imagination' – echoes a number of its uses, particularly those in mathematics, science and philosophy, where it joins synonymous or near-synonymous words such as 'representation', 'diagram' or 'simulacrum'. It describes a selective presentation or depiction of something in a way doesn't exhaust all of the potential attributes or permutations of that thing. We can say that affordance (and therefore aesthetics in general) constitutes or *maps musical objects as corresponding images of music*. In the same way that music space becomes human music space once a locus of human aesthetics structures it, affordance structures certain expected and perceived characteristics of musical objects as images of those objects.

Having said this, images of music aren't precisely or absolutely derived from particular precisely given musical objects. Being structured collections of constrained variables, images are none other than musical objects themselves, technically speaking, and in the same way as with musical objects we can speak of concentric subsets of images making up larger images. Images are musical objects as they appear in the mind, literally, theoretically or potentially: they are 'imaginations' of music. They're what listeners experience in music in place of exhaustively described musical objects themselves, what listeners expect and derive in their minds from the musical performances they hear or hear about. As with affordance, images are themselves dependent on, influenced by or derived from many other images and may in turn give rise to other new images as part of the continual process of adaptive learning described by Gibson.

These images aren't just the preserve of listening: composers refer to and generate images of music as they compose in exactly the way that listeners do as they listen. Composers, remember, don't personally and consciously specify every single piece of possible information (i.e. every degree of freedom), but only attend to some of that information through certain collections of certain variables, which are images of (their) music. Composing, performing and listening are ultimately the same activity: the constituting of images of music. The only difference applies when composers, performers and listeners fall into starkly divided categories during the act of music-making (as they are seen to Western classical music, for example), in which case it lies in their respective freedoms to constitute amounts of musical information (in conventional Western classical music, individual composers have huge freedom to constitute musical information, while other participants, including listeners, have comparatively little). Constituting music is a two-way process, so it's equally the case that these amounts of musical information in turn constitute or create the figure of the composer, performer and listener through their respective domains of information.

Away from actual musical performances, images of music are particular vague sets of understandings, memories and expectations regarding the activity of musical variables which influence how we hear future musical performances. In themselves, images can imply a number of different, 'original' musical objects corresponding to those images, but it may not be easy or possible to tell what the further attributes of these musical objects 'really' are or were, though we can at least say that there are musical objects 'underneath' or *beyond* them. They are the aesthetic constructions (or (re)constitutions) of music, aesthetic 'preparations' of it, and as such are compositions themselves. Like the affordances that drive their construction according to particular interests, images of music are changeable and indeed constantly changing, and differ between listeners, cultures and periods in history.

Images of music tend to apply most notably to more complex musical objects where there's more information to select certain attributes from, and a greater need to do so. One way to think of what images of music are is to imagine them as maps of areas that exist in physical reality. Say we wanted to make a map of part of a country. This land could be hundreds of square miles in area, and the amount of potential information contained in that area would be enormous – buildings, plants, populations of people and animals, topography, geology, economy, transport, history and more, right down to microscopic levels. What's more, all of this information will change over time and at different rates. When we make a map of that area, we have to discriminate between all this information, and reduce it to certain specific features depending on why we're making the map, just as affordance discriminates musical information.

If we wanted to make a geological map, we'd mark the topography of the landscape and the areas where certain rocks are to be found, we wouldn't bother marking the locations of roads, settlements, forests, county borders and such beyond what was practically necessary, and we'd have to give or imply a date at which the map was correct. If we wanted to make a map of population or economy, we'd structure the map differently, shading areas different colours depending on the information we'd gathered, while not bothering about topographical detailing (unless we were trying to show some correlation between topography and economy). If we wanted to make a tourist map, we'd mark on roads, public transport and the names of areas and the places tourists might like to visit. If we were making a map of the area for general use, we'd include a modest amount of all these things. In none of these cases would the map constitute all the possible information about the area 'underneath' or 'beyond' it, and naturally we couldn't say that it 'was' that area, that the two were the same thing. By now we've added a proviso that the constitution of musical objects discussed in Part 2 is not a simple case of constituting systems 'being' those musical objects, but one of the appearance of information: the map doesn't constitute the land itself, but constitutes or creates information about it.

In the same way, images of music reduce all the possible manifestations of information from musical objects to a certain set of features according to affordance. And as Gibson explained, affordance is something built up by and dependent on learning, some of which comes from experience, some of which is learned from others. We can create maps of reality based on this learning, but perceiving an image of music or holding it as an opinion or expectation is often a lot less formal than making a map, even in an unofficial capacity. Sometimes it's little more than a casual idea or assumption about a musical object based on experience. If you were to briefly think of music played on an electric guitar, you would generate an image of the musical object that is 'music played on an electric guitar'. A common image of electric guitar-playing is its capacity to actualise rock music, which it often does. This image was even more common decades ago, before the electric guitar was incorporated into a wider range of musics. Accordingly, if electric guitars are still in use in hundreds of years' time, this image of them may be very different. Even if these future listeners were to think of an image of what they call 'rock music', the average sound of the style may have shifted in the intervening time to something very unlike, say, The Rolling Stones. There is probably a significant extent to which this image of electric guitars is a tendency that applies at a social, cultural and maybe even global level – when many people think of electric guitars, they expect, assume and associate their actuali-sation with a context of rock music. This image of electric guitar playing constrains it towards rock music, despite all its possible actualisations.

If I were to say, 'they walked onto the stage and played electric guitars', you might casually imagine, guess or expect that some sort of rock music was played. This depends on context, of course – both that of the person hearing this sentence, with their background and associations (maybe they've never heard rock music), and the fact that a stage suggests rock music more than other settings might, and that little further qualifying description is given. This is not to say that whoever informally imagines the image of electric guitars as rock music *doesn't know* that electric guitars can do other things, or that they won't be open to discovering that they can play musics other than rock music, or that they'll consciously feel that their expectations had been thwarted, or that they won't even recognise that the electric guitar is being played if it's not rock music. But images like these and how they're modified during performance do affect the ways we perceive musical objects and change in music as if we were reading a map that pointed out certain features rather than, or more than, others.

Let's consider a similar example, this time showing the different images people can come to have of musical works or performances according to their prior expectations. If I were told that I was going to hear a performance by a band that play electric guitars and it turned out that they played compositions by the eighteenth-century classical composer J.S. Bach, I would be surprised. Bach's music is rarely performed on electric guitars. I would find the fact that electric guitars were playing Bach one of the most noticeable, noteworthy and important features of (that is, pieces of information afforded by) the performance. This aspect would contribute to my image of the performance – my assessment of what musical changes held the most significance – because my prior images of electric guitars and of performing Bach had been challenged, the change relative to my prior experience being considerable. I would of course know and accept that electric guitars could physically play Bach if asked beforehand, but this wouldn't alter the surprise. Yet other members of the audience might not find it surprising or particularly noteworthy at all in their images of the performance. Unlike me, they may have already learned that the band were going to play Bach, or they may be very familiar with a whole culture of eighteenth-century music played on electric guitars that I wasn't aware of. Still other listeners – perhaps those not so well versed in Western culture – may have no particular prior images of electric guitars, rock music or Bach in mind, and would perhaps experience the various attributes of the music far more evenly than I had (unless, say, they weren't used to the high volume levels and hated them, in which case their image of the performance would be unlikely to have much to do with texture or harmony, and more to do with the relative 'loudness' they'd perceived).

Each of these different listeners to the performance would construct a different image and thus a different experience and opinion of the performance, depending on their prior images of the musical objects they encountered during the performance. These images would be altered by the performance, some more than others. They may not be able to put these images into language very well or present them in any defined way – in fact the moment they try to talk about or define their experiences, that image is likely to change again, perhaps becoming more specific than it was before. Images can't necessarily be thought of as 'really there' in our minds, ready to be measured. They may only be able to be defined potentially, negatively or differentially. An image of the frequency 440Hz probably won't actually suggest a particular instrument at all, but you're likely to have expected it being actualised by some sound sources, such as a piano, more than others, such as an electric drill. But images of music do nonetheless have an effect on our perception of musical significance and meaning, on music's further affordances – that is, the generation of new images of music.

Images of music structure and are structured by listening. They may not necessarily be simple lists of salient features, but a certain structuring or ordering of perception, an 'aesthetic agenda' concerning what types of change – during the performance or in relation to other performances – are significant. Without images of music, all we hear are disordered sounds (in fact, without the information processing capabilities that create these images for us, our brains wouldn't really be functioning at all). If we were to send the Bach played on electric guitars to some aliens who hadn't heard any other human music and had no knowledge of human culture, they would have no reference point or prior learning, and as a result the images they construct in listening could be wildly different to those that we might construct. None of the meanings and significances that may be afforded for some human listeners to the electric Bach – iconoclasm, irony, experimentation, the eighteenth century, the twentieth century, certain harmonic, melodic or timbral events and far more besides – would be apparent to the aliens. Depending on their brains or equivalents thereof, the aliens could appreciate the sonic qualities of the performance in the same way that we might appreciate the sonic qualities of a language we don't speak (which makes a good metaphor for how we listen to more experimental music relative to music with more culturally established and ingrained significances and meanings). The aliens might even be able to notice certain patterns, structures and internal logics in the pitches, but they would not, so to speak, understand the musical *language* of the performance – its structure of meaning perception – in the way we do, even if it could develop its own.

So the store of images of music we have in or at the backs of our minds, which we've built up in our lifetimes through a developing process driven by learning and affordance, is like a language that we draw on to derive further affordances, meanings and other significances from the musical information we hear. While images are comparable with and could in some cases be connected to words and their definitions in that language, they're usually far more fluid, relative and changeable in relation to musical objects than words are. Neither musical objects nor their images could have a practical universal dictionary of meanings that would be as useful as one for defining words is, for example, although they do structure the perception of and the meanings that arise from listening.

Images of Styles and of Music-itself

Between listenings, images of music have significant effect and importance at the level of musical style. The complexity of styles as musical objects is comparable to that of languages, as is their capacity to unite musical practice and communities around a common or loosely common system of meaning. In the previous two parts I discussed how, as musical objects, styles are often so complex (being spread over many different performances and changing or repeating variables and values in many detailed ways) that the only way to think of them is as loosely verifiable statistical patterns, where using mere linguistic labels (such as 'jazz') were relatively weak for defining a style space. This is because the extent to which we can only know them as reduced to images is much greater than it is with simpler musical objects. All we really experience about styles are the images that only imperfectly imply a musical object beyond them, images that may not be statistically verifiable (i.e. somewhat more objective) at all. Styles as we know them tend to be tied to discrete concepts that are often named by words, and as images these are only impressionistic and changeable structures of certain features and certain variabilities.

Like any other image, images of styles reduce the information content of styles according to context. The eighteenth-century classical style of Bach has a number of features, but at the time only some of them were taken into account. It was practically taken for granted that this style was performed on orchestral instruments, pitch and duration were quantised, with each piece at a fairly regular tempo and volume, and so these elements were practically undetected or subordinate according to the contemporary images of that style. These images constituted and appreciated melodies, harmonies and textures more than other characteristics, such as timbres and volumes. Though they could have done, listeners familiar with the context and language of Bach's style would be unlikely to marvel at, be bored with or particularly notice at all the way the pulse, volume and timbres are consistent, or the way that pitch and duration is chopped into a relatively small number of discrete values, since these attributes could be taken for granted. They were not part of (or not prominent in) the perception and appreciation of the style as structured by its image. To a more distant observer, such as one in the early twenty-first century, the image of Bach's style appears to adopt more features relative to other styles we know, such as its being played on what is today just a particular subset of musical instruments, an aspect which might be brought into relief in an age of electrical instruments. On the other hand, for some listeners today it may lose some of its more complex features, such as various details of its harmonic language that listeners were better able to recognise, follow or ascribe meaning to at the time.

At that time, any form of musical change outside of the locus of that image was felt to be 'wrong' or difficult to imagine as appealing. Had Bach written an atonal (i.e. without a key) and microtonal (i.e. using pitch intervals smaller than the semitones most Western music is quantised to) unmeasured (i.e. without bars or *metre* – measured time) fugue for seven specific fretless stringed instruments he'd just invented, each painted in a different colour of the rainbow, and that should only be performed outside on a Friday afternoon, listeners would not just have had their expectations thwarted. They would probably struggle to appreciate the work as just another musical composition by the same Bach, because their image of his music and the musical style of the time had been so violently challenged. Alongside the unconventional nature of the sounds and ensemble, strictly and personally specifying the colours and locations of the instruments in time and space simply wasn't done (and is still rarely done today). The work would have offered barely any of the culturally expected affordances. More likely, most listeners would not even think of the work as proper 'music' at all. They'd probably consider Bach to have gone mad and react to him accordingly, unless he was somehow able to make a persuasive enough defence of his new work. I mean this last point quite seriously: an inability or unwillingness to observe and comply with the implicit images regulating the perception and aesthetics of art and life in general was classified as madness or put down to limited or altered mental capacity in many eras, and judgements of this kind persist to this day.

Today an atonal, microtonal and unmeasured fugue could be well received in many contexts, and relatively few in the West would deny that the work was actually music (probably on the basis of hearing stringed instruments), even if they didn't happen to like it. Even in contemporary classical music, microtones and unmeasured scores are rare, and the specification of colours for the instruments and a time of day for the performance would be more likely to be written off as a relative eccentricity than taken seriously, with some more narrow-minded and territorial commentators classifying it as the province of performance art rather than music because of such features. But the fact that some of Bach's listeners would not have considered a microtonal fugue to be 'music' at all suggests that there are also *images of music-itself*. Bach's 'mad' fugue would sit happily within the locus of many people's images of music-itself today, even if it'd probably be quite far from the centre of that image. But images of music-itself have a significant effect on people's judgements about music today, and are in evidence when people argue over what is or isn't 'music', or 'good music' in particular.

In an absolute sense, 'underneath' or 'beyond' these images, such discussion is meaningless – both 'music' and 'good music' are relative categories with no absolute definition. Many people, though, wouldn't consider noise music to be 'music' or 'good music' due to the restrictions in their image of music-itself. They may express this view explicitly, or simply find it less valuable or comparable to other music. From the point of view of music space it is no more or less 'music' or 'good music' than any other musical object. Similarly, I expect that many of the readers of this book will find that my insistence on music's non-sonic components and their importance will contravene their images of music-itself, maybe to the point where they disagree with me. Perhaps I'm even 'mad' to some extent, like Bach in the example.

Images of music and of music-itself may allow that many kinds of music are possible, may even allow that music has (virtually) infinite possibilities, but they can still have an appreciable effect on musical aesthetics. Remember that an image is not usually a simple black-and-white list of features that are either 'inside' the image or 'outside' of it, or a list of dos and don'ts. They're orderings of perceptions, aesthetic priorities, assumptions and expectations, and they average out over time as tendencies and cultural beliefs. Even ostensibly broad-minded figures such as contemporary or experimental composers, musicologists and music critics often turn out to hold specific images of music or music-itself, the priorities of which they or their audiences may not be entirely aware of. Such images are rarely explicitly given. So often when we hear the phrase 'new music', for example, the implied image fails to live up to the true breadth of the term. The entirety of human music space is not at all presented equally at many concerts advertised as 'new music', rather it's reduced to a certain set of aesthetic priorities and it transpires 'new music' really means 'new [classical] music'.[43] In many contexts the word 'music' often really means [classical] music, or [conventional Western] music in this way. Many educational courses labelled 'composition' betray such an image of composition as [classical] composition, and can only welcome and tolerate non-classical composition to a limited extent.

Similarly, the image (literally, in many cases) of the composer in Western culture is often one of a studious, brooding and reserved white male, clad smartly in black, or else a historical one of a white male eighteenth-century European in a powdered wig, or someone resembling Beethoven, all of whom write music for violins, oboes, horns and other orchestral instruments. 'Composers' are really [classical] composers and not simply whoever creates music. The composer may turn out be a woman in ripped jeans, and we (hopefully) wouldn't be unable to perceive or recognise that she was a composer, but nonetheless this recognition wouldn't mean we hadn't held a particular image of composers in mind. Were I to call a rapper, an improvising saxophonist or a rock band 'composers', most people would instinctively feel that I'd used the term incorrectly. Many would even assume that using the word 'composer' for these musical figures was a compliment, a positive value-judgement, because according to our cultural image of composers they are more 'artistic' and valuable than other kinds of musicians. Needless to say, these images stand in the way of our imagining music and musicians as potentially equal and continuous with each other.

Musical Canons

So images of music direct our perception of what it is that constitutes particular musical objects – especially at the level of style, that is, our opinions and assumptions concerning how musical change will operate between performances – and even what constitutes musical activity itself. In this way, images of music have very real consequences for the way we judge aesthetic value in music, and as such can have a detrimental effect on the ability to appreciate and even imagine music that doesn't fit to their templates.

The word *canon* is used to express a set of rules or principles dictating 'good taste' or aesthetic value. Appropriately enough, the term also describes the set of works within a particular field that are considered to be of the highest standard, or at least recognised and accepted as valid. Literature and philosophy have canons, and a famous musical canon is that of Western classical music, which can either be thought of as a list of works or as an ordering of all work according to how likely they are to be performed. In accordance with the close identification of the figures of Western composers with their works, canons are very often presented as made up of composers themselves. Bach, Beethoven and Brahms are said to form the core of this canon, while Mozart, Schubert and Wagner are not far behind. These composers don't need first names any more. Note the relationship to the word 'canonise', too – these are figures that have been culturally anointed as musical saints. There are sub-canons too: canons of French, Scandinavian and Eastern European classical music, canons of sacred music or eighteenth-century music, canons of music for particular instruments. Accounts of the contents of canons change from person to person but apply at a cultural level as average tendencies which themselves can shift over time. Although their importance is still recognised by historians, composers such as Guillaume de Machaut and Christoph Willibald Glück at certain times seemed a lot more famous and canonical than they are today, while composers such as Gustav Mahler and Charles Ives have become relatively more canonical since their deaths. We could say that other styles, such as jazz, rock, dance music and many non-Western styles have their own canons too.

Such canons are not just lists, but play a role as value-orientated images of music applying at a cultural level. The word 'canon' comes from a Greek word for 'measuring rod', and there is a very real sense in which non-canonical musical works and musical objects in general are measured against the canon. Canons amount to aesthetic filtration processes, automatic value-judgement machines that compare works with an image of 'good taste' or 'worthwhile music' and render those that don't measure up as both unworthy and practically invisible. People don't always realise that a canon only amounts to a *certain* mode of appreciation, a *certain* way of listening and not an aesthetic absolute, just as a map always has a specific range of uses in mind. The Western classical music canon only has certain affordances, certain aesthetic uses in mind, and it can obscure (as in both occlude and, more metaphorically, make obscure) other forms of music and listening that can be equally appealing but in different ways. While listening to a range of classical music may enhance our musical imaginations, holding the Western classical music canon to be an image of music or of total music space will, to a significant extent, restrict both composers' and listeners' imaginations of music space to its own particular – and narrow – aesthetic locus.

Modern Music (Music Beyond Images)

All images of music, and not just those we might term canons, can come to have this *canonical effect* of constraining the aesthetic imagination. An image of jazz is a certain limited idea of 'jazzness', an image of the electric guitar is a certain limited idea of 'electric guitar-ness', an image of melody is a certain limited idea of 'melodiness' and an image of music-itself is a certain limited idea of 'musicness'. All of these '-nesses' are insufficient descriptions, imaginations and (re)constitutions of the musical objects that could be beyond them. They're all certain opinions as to 'essences' that are not absolute or absolute reality but maps with particular, limited uses in mind that will not recognise or constitute certain features as much as others.

Images of music have blind spots. If images of music are what regulate our perception of change in musical information, then some types of change will be recognised more than others. What's more, some types of change may be all too recognisable and will afford negative reactions, such as the removal of key, metre and pitch quantisation and the unfamiliar instruments in the 'mad Bach' example, or the presence of features that may have negative associations. Because of this, images of music can be an obstacle to the production and appreciation of genuinely new music, and composers are pitted against them when they compose new music. Listening according to an insufficient image can be thought of as listening in the wrong dimensions (i.e. using the wrong variables): if the image of some particular music you hold to be valid is that the music varies in two dimensions A and B, and some composers produce new music that varies in dimensions B and C, you'll only be able to constitute the music as one-dimensional. You'll miss A, and you'll only find the music half as appreciable. If composers do branch out into new dimensions, such an image of music may prevent this novelty being appreciated or noticed at all. Even if in the West the authority of musical tradition and convention is weaker than ever before and modern technology has given us more access to music space than ever before, the more subtle, unconscious and ubiquitous authority of images of music can still threaten to obscure or extinguish genuinely new and potentially appreciable musical innovation, both today and tomorrow.

It's only half the battle, then, for composers to compose new music. Listening equates to composing in that both activities constitute musical information, so without an appropriate way of listening – an appropriately adapted image of music – new music will not appear new, viable or recognisable at all. The capacity to recognise new music, in particular, is a problem in an age of post-experimental music, in which the strictures of tradition and convention were discarded many decades ago and it's often difficult to feel that anything new can truly be created, that any relevant difference can be made. But this is only a certain image of 'new music', and one that survives from a previous age into ours: new music as the absolute dismantling of convention rather than any adoption of new and unusual conventions. The newness of this post-experimental music could be subtle, detailed and complex rather than starkly evident. If new music (or different music in general) is to be appreciated, then it has to be received through *new ways of listening*. Indeed, the dichotomy is largely false because the two activities both constitute music: new music *is* new listening, and new listening *is* new music.

So it's not just up to composers to identify and overcome their images of music. Listeners must do this too if they want to experience music *as* new – whether it's new music itself or old music with a fresh perspective. Of course, a preference for freshness in music is itself a certain image of music, but the need to keep our imaginations working and constantly adapting to pastures new – musically or generally – is vital to our well-being and improvement as individuals, as societies and as cultures. Music space can be seen as both the destination and the source of this process in music, which we can call *modernism*. All images of music are reductions of and constraints on the infinity and absolute equality of music space. Images are less than music space: music space exceeds images, it lies beyond them. But of course images are unavoidable – we need them in order to experience any information in music at all. Yet given the role of images as describing systems that reconstitute musical objects, we can constantly strive for better, more accurate, more detailed images of music, images that have a better fidelity to music space and its sub-spaces – better maps of music space. This process is achieved through, or at least in metaphorical parallel with, the development and usage of *modern* technology and scientific discovery, and reflects *modernity*. Modernity is constantly 'beyond' images, one step ahead of them, and as such necessitates the creation of new images that better reflect the changed possibilities and structures of the modern world.

Composers, listeners, performers and anyone who constitutes music (they all do the same thing) accomplish this by better revealing the infinite and continuous music space beyond images of music, which was called 'dequantisation' at the end of Part 1. This allows the creation of new music and, in turn, modern music. Music space itself can't be revealed in its entirety – it is infinite after all – but more detailed or simply different images of music, constituting and accumulating more musical information (as information-bearing degrees of freedom) can bring it into ever sharper focus (as per the progressive specification of musical objects). In this way the musical objects that go unobserved or unappreciated because of the restrictions of images can be revealed, and more information can be added to our maps of music, increasing our perception of its reality.

Music Criticism and Music-as-music-criticism

One effective way of doing this is through *music criticism*, or writing about or discussing music in general. Because writing about music constitutes information about music, music criticism can be thought of as a form of musical composition and as such an art form in itself. It creates new images of music, bringing new or different images of new musical objects into them in the same way that composers create musical objects. Music criticism may or may not overlap with music journalism, but it can't be reduced to the judgement of musical value (which we could call *reviewing*) or the determination of causes for particular musical objects (which we could call *explanation*) that are also to be found in music journalism. Music criticism *shows*, while reviewing and explanation contribute to constraining or territorialising images of music. Most writing about music has some inseparable mixture of all three categories, of course, but a criticism that on average expands the aesthetic images held by its readers, rather than (re)enforcing them, is a criticism that creates a path to modern music.

Writing about music can only go so far, however, because of its dependency on the limitations of language. Music itself is in many respects a suppler and more finely grained system of meaning, and if music criticism equates to musical composition, then surely musical composition can equate to music criticism. Music, then, can itself act as a describing system for other

musical objects revealing new information that wasn't constituted by the old images. New musical objects can 'play up to'
images of other musical objects but modify, expand or exceed
them, demonstrating what was relatively less perceptible before
and functioning themselves as a fresh way of listening. Like
music criticism, however, this *music-as-music-criticism* can easily
slide into (re)enforcing images of music on average, and as such
can cease to offer new information and even offer less. Music-as-
music-criticism has often been thought of as *postmodern music*,
but if such music offers a new or technologically aware way of
listening to music, it can to some degree attest to modernity.

A recent trend in Western concrete music often given the name
'hauntology', for example, has revealed the technological frailty
of vinyl and tape recordings alongside historical musical styles in
ways that were generally less appreciated when they were still
relatively recent.[44] This is largely because at the time their
technological shortcomings were normally 'listened-through' and
barely detected, taken for granted, or even actively disliked and
discarded. Hauntology's composers revealed this by using tape
noise, vinyl crackle and musical form in ways that would have
seemed 'excessive' or difficult to imagine as appealing according
to the images of that music that had applied at the time or to date.
Though at times this music arguably serves to (re)enforce images
of music through nostalgia (the 'rose-tinted spectacles' of which
are often the sentiment that creates constraining, territorialising
images of music *par excellence*), its ironic fidelity nonetheless
overturns the canons of listening and attests to previously
unappreciated musical objects. This is the case whether they're
the sonic by-products of imperfect technology, or whole styles
and forms of music-making that had been forgotten by
mainstream music history. The music is rich in wider cultural
meanings alongside its purely sonic interests.

A Definition of New Music

This process of revealing music space, then, is one of adding to or modifying the discriminate information (information selectively assembled through affordance) that makes up images of music in order to create new images with new affordances. It's the same as the process as the progressive specification of music discussed in the last part. This progressive specification was an increasing ability to constitute musical objects through a net increase in the number of information-bearing degrees of freedom. New music demands a *net* or overall, average increase in these degrees of freedom. If the number of degrees of freedom in the image remained roughly the same or even decreased but bore different information, this would still amount to new music if this new information were added alongside that of the previous, unchanged image. It would contribute to an increase in information for the listener in the same way that the aliens of Part 2 accumulated information about jazz by hearing more and more jazz performances.

We could consider this net increase in specified musical information, or the freedom to constitute specific new musical information through the adding of new degrees of freedom, to be a definition of new music. It can apply relative to a particular image of music – that is, limited to a particular music-making context or musical object, 'new to jazz', 'new to piano-playing', a new version of a musical work – or to perceptions of music space as a whole. Technically speaking this 'increase' describes new*er* music: a relative movement directed towards new music, heading into uncharted areas of music space from the position of whatever was previously relatively familiar.

Thus creating new music could mean widening the range of musical variables in a musical object (or its image), which increases the overall degree of freedom, or adding new constrained variables to a musical object (or its image), which increases the overall number of degrees of freedom. So according to this definition, 'new music' can mean as little as the switching of a single 0 to a 1 in a sample of computer-generated music (white noise perhaps), or the adding of a new bit at any point in its binary code. Thus altering a single pitch in a pre-existing musical work by a tenth of a hertz could create new music. The change that new music requires is arbitrarily small. That 'new music' can have such a minute definition is a reflection of the idea that we can't step into the same river twice. The analogy describes how the universe is constantly changing, and constantly new because of it. Music is the same, it's constant, continuous change. It's all new, all the time and at any time.

Obviously this is no consolation for those who, like myself, feel that a sufficient degree of novelty is often lacking in some areas of musical culture. You couldn't plan a new music festival for human listeners around simply changing or adding a few bits of information to music files here and there, or adjusting a single pitch by a hair's breadth. All music festivals, in fact, would be 'new music' festivals whatever music was played, since the values of some variables would have changed from previous performances. This simply means that new music is relative, but that doesn't mean we can't talk about it.

Clearly computer bits and other arbitrarily small changes are too insignificant for an adequate definition of new music. It would be wrong (not to mention difficult) to create an absolute definition of exactly how much new information is sufficient to award the title of 'new music', however. Images of musical novelty should be flexible enough to suit whatever context it arises in. Returning to arbitrary change, then, we can qualify our definition of new music by saying that the new information added to the image of music must *afford a perception of sufficient novelty* for listeners. This new information must appear to listeners in units scaled up to an 'affordable' size, which will obviously vary depending on the listener and the context. In typical sound files, computer bits are too small to afford musical novelty (or even lead to humanly perceptible change at all), but other musical objects constituted in human music space, such as slightly different harmonies or melodies, may also be too minor to be sufficient. Because the 'size' of these units of useful information (i.e. these degrees of freedom) will vary, all we can say for sure is that the more new degrees of freedom there are, the 'newer' the music is, and the more music space will be suggested. I would encourage an increase in new degrees of freedom as high as it's possible to afford, but it's a definition of new music with flexibility built into it.

Critical Listening

The (relative) progressive specification of music is how musical information is constituted, differentiated, made new, and ultimately actualised. It applies to both composers and listeners equally – when we listen to music, we progressively specify it across time according to affordance (both the music's capacities and ours, affordance is a two-way process), gathering more and more information until we've got what we need, or we become distracted, or the musical performance comes to an end. This means that if we gather more information than we did on a previous occasion while listening to the same musical object, we'd be constituting new music. We'd be performing the same role as music criticism in that we'd be revealing more information about music (space) to ourselves. We could call this form of listening *critical listening*, and its definition is nothing more complex than 'listening more carefully so as to gather more information'. Again, this 'more' is relative and arbitrarily small, it can be scaled up to an appropriate degree.

Critical listening employs a listener's ability to constitute a more detailed image of music and thus reveal more of music space. That listening more carefully to music is more informative and leads to the discovery of new musical objects is intuitively true, of course. But I would emphasise the point that new music is often discovered by listening carefully rather than superficially, and won't become immediately obvious 'in the music itself' or in the first image of it. The novelty of music may not lie in the variables and values than can easily be detected as soon as the music begins to play (of which timbre or style are good examples for today's Western listeners), but in any kind (i.e. variable) of musical change, however subtle. Musical novelty may not be as immediately obvious as it often was in the twentieth century, although the change to be constituted could still be profoundly significant and appreciable. Making musical novelty loud and clear to a listener is not a bad thing at all – far from it, as it can greatly and easily freshen our imaginations and galvanise composition, debate and new ways of listening. But if this sort (this image) of new music is seen as the rule, significant musical novelty will often be missed entirely.

This is not to say that critical listening is necessarily more complex or detailed listening. It can in fact be the opposite. Sometimes a simpler image of music is what is needed to dequantise the highly specific, language-like ways of listening we've developed over time and reveal the breadth of music space's possibility. Listening carefully to music may amount not to the determination of ever more detailed structures, but to the discovery of a much simpler, more sensual experience. This is something Cage, who was influenced by Zen Buddhist philosophy, understood when he dequantised the ornate habits of Western music into a simple space of continuous pitches, timbres, durations, volumes and morphologies.

Paradoxically, however, it's often assumed that the twentieth-century music of Cage's contemporaries will afford the same amount of information and the same complex and profound significance that was associated with nineteenth-century music as typified by the likes of Beethoven. Quite often it can, of course, but very often the basic fact of modernist music's dequantisation into pure variability is an important aspect of its appreciation.

This is actually a much easier path to twentieth-century music than the myth, perpetuated by composers and critics alike, that it must be listened to with stoical concentration and perseverance. A work by Beethoven could potentially be constituted and experienced through thousands of degrees of freedom, but remember that Cage's sound space only needed five, and yet in this it encompassed more of music space than any other system of the time. Each degree of freedom had a broader, purer locus of variability than the more complex, more specific, 'higher' structures of more stylised, language-like musical traditions. Careful listening can be dequantised listening, a listening that constitutes atonality as pure pitch rather than the advanced language of the new Bach. As a visual analogy that corresponds, appropriately, to that used in Part 2 to illustrate the progressive specification of musical objects, this way of listening constitutes all the simple beauty of the colour blue, without the inundation of all planet Earth's information. But both the simpler and more complex routes of critical listening have an equal power and capacity for new music, and somewhere between these two extremes lie all critical experiences of music.

Repetition, Difference and Images of Music

We can think of critical listening as being one instance of a more general principle that facilitates the gathering of musical information and the generation of new images of music: *repetition*. Critical listening can be achieved through experiencing repeated performances of the same musical object (repeatedly playing the same musical work, for example, especially in new contexts or after new information has been learned), or repeatedly or more regularly 'sampling' information about the music during the performance. In these ways, music can be made to repeat itself at the discretion of a listener, allowing them to gather as much information as they can or would like. But this process of informative repetition is also something that composers can have control over, of course. It can be used to make new or otherwise atypical forms of specific musical information more accessible and perceptible to listeners.

Repetition is fundamental to music and its greatest asset. Its importance in aiding musical appreciation is regularly underestimated in the aesthetics of Western art music, whose increasing information-richness (both at the level of works and overall musical milieu) has often been in need of its ability to clarify and familiarise musical objects. Repetition doesn't just mean the repetition of melodies, melodic fragments, rhythms, the 'cells' of minimalist music or entire musical passages across the single discrete time continuums set up by a single musical work, although this does have the desired effect. It can also mean repetition *between* these time continuums: between performances, between musical works, between instruments, between musical styles, and between all musical objects, where it has the same effect of building, consolidating and cohering musical information. And here, repetition can mean both the recurrence of a discrete musical object across time (a repeated guitar riff, for example), or a musical object continuously remaining the same over time (such as a droning pitch or a constant volume level).

All constrained variables (i.e. all musical objects) can be repeated, even those we don't conventionally think of as repeating. A work for solo violin may not repeat a single pitch value at all throughout its duration, but the timbre value (i.e. that of a violin) would effectively repeat with every new note, or simply remain the same continuously in time, which is the same thing. The same reverb settings can be applied to multiple musical works or performances. Certain time durations themselves can repeat across longer durations, which is how we experience a regular subdivided pulse, with the length of a crotchet, say, repeating itself constantly across a longer length of time. Values don't just have to repeat across time continuums – they could repeat across a pitch continuum, for example. A single timbre value could repeat at different pitches to form a chord where all timbres are played at the same time, although such a form of repetition is a little harder for the average listener to detect than repetition across time. If a value is perceived not to repeat or remain the same it's perceived to *differ*. In that music is a complex system of variables, it is a complex system of repetition and difference where what appears to repeat and what differs, and by how much (i.e. at what relative rates), is always in flux.

However, we've already noted that music and the world in which it exists are in constant change, and are constantly new. This novelty is arbitrarily small, and can take place infinitesimally along the continuous path of any variable. How, then, can music be said to repeat or remain the same at all? It can't repeat entirely, of course, because some possible variable or degree of freedom can always be said to differ at the point of performance. But it can be *perceived* as repeating in two senses. Firstly musical objects can be perceived to repeat if we discount certain variables and the values they might have. If we perform the same musical work on two occasions and in two different locations and we discount the variables of time and location (which we conventionally do), then we usually say we've repeated the musical work. But if we counted location values as a defining feature of the work, we wouldn't be able to say we'd repeated the work, at least to the same extent. This repetition is the product of perception only: the discounting of variables or values is the same discrimination and discounting of musical information that generates an image of music (i.e. affordance). In discounting certain variables and values, we've created a certain image of the work, and it's that image that repeats in place of all the information that can possibly be constituted at the point of the actual, infinitely concrete performance.

Secondly, and more correctly, variables may not be fully discounted but may rather change their values at slower rates relative to other variables. Performances can't ever be said to repeat or remain the same, but they can instead be said to differ at a slower or otherwise less noticeable rate. The timbre of a solo violin doesn't *actually* stay the same at the concrete level because there are minute differences in small acoustic values between each note (because we can't step into the same violin twice). But these differences are small and perceptibly negligible relative to the difference in the pitch variable. We perceive the timbre as staying the same *relative to* the pitch, when in actual reality it's just changing at a different, 'slower' or subtler rate.

Or we may perceive the different rates of change adequately but still acknowledge the difference, say if one violin changed pitch at a rate of forty times per minute, another at eighty and another at a hundred and sixty. On average the violin changing at forty beats per minute differs less across the variable of time than the other two, and we can put that somewhat paradoxically, saying that it 'remained the same *more*' than the other two. Because of its slow rate of change, the slowest violin would on average have constituted less information over an arbitrary length of time relative to the others. So images can be thought of as either 'discounting' degrees of freedom or setting up differential relations between collections of variables regarding their relative amounts of changing information. But both these senses still amount to the same process, that of discriminating and ordering musical information to create an image of music.

In the last part we saw how we come to 'know' musical objects because they recur. Now we can say more specifically that we come to form *images* of those musical objects because they recur. Every image of music is a certain way of constituting what changes and what stays the same and by how much, what differs and what repeats and at what relative rate of difference. Since all music can be thought of as perpetual difference of information that can only be fully understood at a single point of infinite concreteness (or where all the degrees of freedom have been constituted at the outermost limit of our physically constrained universe's capacity to do so), we can't say that we truly have the measure of musical objects independently of images unless we're outside the physical constraints of the universe and observing every single bit of information in it. Instead, we can constitute more information than previous images of music did by creating better images, (re)constituting music anew, recounting the variables and values we discounted and noticing rates of change we hadn't done before.

It's repetition that does this by developing its images, bringing them into clearer focus and increasing information. Again, this one process can be thought to happen in two senses, even if they're ultimately the same. Firstly, it allows the listener to derive further information about what is perceived as 'the same' (information-discounted) musical object by keeping it fixed in place and allowing a listener to scrutinise it further. Eventually, what repeats will come to stand out against whatever differs, forming an image of what is repeated that's independent from everything that changes. After this, some amount of subsequent difference may then be enough to afford the creation of a new, differentiated image.

Secondly, since all repetition is not actually concrete repetition but includes some degree of difference across some variable (even if that difference is nothing more than in time, i.e. the relative location within a broader time continuum, such as that of life itself), repetition thus equates to difference and will thus inevitably change our image of a musical object by adding new variables or values with each repetition. Repetition creates images of music for the listener but can also change them, or to put it more accurately: *repetition simultaneously creates and changes images of music*. Again, what changes (what is revealed, which is new) and what doesn't (what is (re)enforced, which was old) and by how much will be perceived as an image by the listener according to affordance. This word 'simultaneously' may make repetition sound like some confusing paradox, but the selfsame constrained variable can't both remain in its entirety *and* change, but rather some constrained variables change while others stay the same or change at a slower rate, but all are contained in the same developing image of music.

Through repetition, music 're-samples' itself, and in doing this it creates and demonstrates images of itself to listeners. But it also has the power to change what is repeated and better reveal information about musical objects 'beyond' the old images. By means of this back-and-forth tension of repetition and difference a single musical work becomes its own music-as-music-criticism, listening critically to itself, adding information to the images it suggests to listeners and developing them. For example, in its capacity as music-as-music-criticism, hauntology repeated the music of the past, sampling it but highlighting new information the second time around, most notably vinyl crackle, tape hiss and other anachronisms both technological and stylistic. This repetition-with-difference may have been inspired by the recently increased availability of CD-quality audio playback, which had meant that listeners no longer 'listened through' crackle and hiss, largely intending to ignore it as they had done before. On occasions when listeners did return to the old music, the crackle and hiss suddenly stood out as an obvious and interesting aspect of the image because it had been absent on the higher quality audio. This interest was reflected in the newly produced music, where hiss and crackle was celebrated and was regularly even stronger than it had been in the past. The hauntology aesthetic creates both a new way of listening to old music and a new music in which the old is repeated with its difference emphasised. The two inform and support each other in a feedback loop that brings about new ways of listening. This repetition-with-difference effect took place over many years of history, caused by the differential of historical change, but it can happen across the length of time set up by individual performances too.

To illustrate this and these difficult notions of repeating and differing images in general, let's imagine a musical example. Say a musical work repeats a musical object, a sequence of pitches (*a, b, c, d*) eight times consecutively. There are many ways to divide the work so far into other musical objects – (*a, b, c*), (*d, a, b*), (*c, d, a*), for example. But the listener comes to perceive a certain object, an image of four pitches (*a, b, c, d*), because that sequence repeats so often, thus the music relatively affords that image *as a grouped unit*. It appears to the listener as a discrete, self-contained locus of change. Now say that at the ninth repetition the fourth pitch changes, so that the sequence is now (*a, b, c, e*), and this repeats eight times. Because the image (*a, b, c, d*) had become so ingrained, the listener is likely to hear this as new information added to the same image (*a, b, c, d*) so that it becomes a musical object that actualises as two sets of pitches rather than just one: (*a, b, c, d/e*). *e* is now included within its locus of variability. In this way, the image (*a, b, c, d*) develops through repetition and difference to become (*a, b, c, d/e*): the *a, b* and *c* repeated, but the *d* differed.

Images of music are not a simple matter of being the same or being different from each other, however. Listening doesn't neatly divide into discrete images of music, as we know from experience – these images of music are only partly separable according to their varying degrees of relative differentiation. (*a, b, c, d*) and (*a, b, c, e*) were not *exactly* the same image, even for the listener, they were just not particularly differentiated. If (*a, b, c, d*) had been recurring on two very different timbres, with (*a, b*) on one timbre and (*c, d*) on another, then (*a, b, c, d*) may well have divided into those two slightly more separated or differentiated images of musical objects. In this case when *e* arrives (if it had the same timbre as *c*) it would more likely be the image (*c, d*) that developed new information, becoming (*c, e*), while (*a, b*) remained the same.

If an entirely new musical object, a sequence of pitches (w, x, y, z), followed (a, b, c, d/e) then the listener may form an entirely new image, but to what degree this image is different or similar would depend on the affordance of that difference. If (w, x, y, z) only differed from (a, b, c, d/e) in a barely perceptible way, if its pitches were only a microtone higher for example, the listener would be unlikely to form a new, more separate image because for them (w, x, y, z) is hardly very differentiated from (a, b, c, d/e), although the difference may have been appreciated to some degree. On the other hand, if (w, x, y, z) was several octaves above (a, b, c, d/e) in pitch, it would afford a difference of much greater significance from (a, b, c, d/e) and would thus be very differentiable from it, so the listener would be likely to form a more separated image of that object. But neither image would be entirely and easily separated and discrete, both images would still be related as sub-images, differentiated to varying extents, within the same overall image of the whole musical performance.

So this image of the musical work can't be divided into separable, discrete images, but rather sub-images that are more or less differentiable relative to one another according to affordance. When we hear a repeating image of music, we don't hear it as *either* repetition *or* difference, but we have a simultaneous and changeable awareness of both to varying extents. Remember that an image of music isn't necessarily a black-and-white list of certain discrete attributes and musical objects – in this case it's a continuous topography marked by varying rates of perceived relative difference giving rise to loosely defined areas of greater and lesser perceived differentiability (sub-images). This, of course, is exactly how human aesthetics (i.e. affordance) turned music space into human music space. Music space became a map where despite their richness of difference for a computer, white noises were hardly differentiable from each other at all (they effectively become the *same*, *repeated* image) relative to more conventional music.

Here we arrive at a final definition for images of music. Images of music are structures of differentiated musical objects; they are differentiations of the continuous flow of musical information into relatively discrete musical objects. This process of differentiation in listening is achieved by means of the progressive specification of information through increasing degrees of freedom, and can take any path through any variables, values and sub-images according to affordance. It applies at all levels of musical listening (and musicking generally), from hearing individual works to reacting to whole styles and cultures of music, and the relative differences and similarities they constitute. It is informed by assumptions and expectations borne of prior experience or learning and happens both during listening and away from actual musical performances, dictating the way we perceive differentiation in musical culture as a whole. This path is a *way* of listening, and forms an image of music.

The Recurring Specifics of Style

When particular musical attributes recur between discrete musical performances, we sometimes loosely collect these attributes together as a certain image of music that we then consider to be a musical style in just the same way that we group together less complex images of music as differentiated units during individual musical performances. We know each style as a certain pattern of repetition (or what changes at a negligible rate and is relatively less differentiable) and difference (or what changes at a noticeable rate and is relatively more differentiable – this change can be internal to a musical performance, relative to something newly presented within it, or a change relative to a listener's past experience of musical performances). The element of repetition forms and loosely holds these images of style together through what we can call *the recurring specifics of style*.

We normally only consider certain classes of recurring

specifics to comprise musical styles: melodies are different but timbres and the accompanying rhythms are repeated, for example, or harmonies are different but tempos repeat or are relatively similar to each other. Many of a style's recurring specifics will have a more complex, detailed structure of certain named or unnamed musical objects and more or less likelihood of certain values or structures recurring, such as certain preferred melodic intervals, timbre combinations, effects and overall temporal form. There's no absolute reason for the concept of style to conform to such predictable patterns of repetition and difference, however. Composers of new music would do well to unsettle these images of 'stylicity' by varying which kinds of musical objects remain the same or repeat and which kinds differ. Anything at all can repeat or differ in bizarre, unexpected and highly specific ways between musical performances and thus be considered part of a style. New images of styles with novel dimensionalities can be created and consolidated for listeners by means of their recurring specifics.

The recurring specifics of style are a particularly important arena for the repetition and difference of music, because they take place across the relatively longer stretches of time and space between performances and thus span our lives. While repetition and difference within a single individual musical performance occurs within a specific time continuum that effectively finishes with the end of the performance, the repetition and difference that makes up musical styles transcend that to apply across a much broader timeframe. Styles divide into many discrete performances, each occurring in different places and at different times, interspersed throughout our lives and at our discretion. This amounts to a much richer form of musical engagement because it puts music back into the course of life as opposed to reducing it to a series of discrete events within it. This quantisation doesn't apply to style, allowing us to live within the repetition and difference of music. If we see music as a continuous system of variables that is in turn continuous with life in a larger sense, then this isn't just a metaphor but another way in which the repetition-with-difference of music takes place for listeners. The only difference is in the conventions of how we divide music as an event into what we think of as separated or relatively differentiated lengths of time, just as musical performances themselves are relatively quantised during the image-making process that is listening, and this division can be dequantised back into the broader continuity of life 'outside' the performance. Style is a musical object just like any other, it just happens to stretch across a broader time continuum as opposed to the single discrete time continuums we call performances. Music itself, and style particularly, doesn't cease to exist when we think of a performance as finished – it's happening all the time.

Style is like a specific language or dialect used in our daily lives, constantly developing and manifesting anew in different contexts, while a single musical performance independent of its capacity for style is little more than a language learned and then discarded. And like a language, style spans a whole community or culture of the different people involved in it, rather than just the individual composers that traditionally create musical works. It allows a variety of individuals to contribute to its development through many forms of participation, be it composition, performance, critical discussion, dancing or even just listening (which is participation too). Style is a musical object composed as a democratic collaboration by a dynamic community spanning time and space. Most importantly, musical style is like a language because it affords a significant degree of shared communal or cultural meaning relevant to our lives. Style is where meaning arises – even, and especially, complex and specific meanings. If this meaning should harden into an image of music through too much of the (re)enforcement of repetition, it's through that image's status *as a style* that it may be conquered, developed and made new (or else differentiated into a relatively or entirely new style) through difference, thus expanding to new affordances and meanings and renewing the imaginations of its listeners.

The recurring specifics of style unite disparate musical performances, unite musical development with that of our general lives, unite groups of people and unite music with the non-sonic meanings it embodies. Because of all this it's a much more significant, even crucial form of repetition-with-difference than that which occurs in musical works or any other single time continuum. Musical style is the most sociable kind of musical object, both because its recurring specifics cohere musical information and meaning for listeners and because it's developed relatively democratically. By contrast, in the Western art music of the nineteenth and twentieth centuries, the standalone musical work was much more the focus of music-making, while styles and instruments were subordinate to the work. This hierarchy of categories is just one limited image of music-itself, of course. Perhaps it's time to challenge the musical work's primacy as being solipsistic, withdrawn from our lives and communities, and move to a new paradigm where works, styles and instruments (and ultimately all musical objects) may vary in their significance and their patterns of repetition and difference, but are on an equal footing overall.

Of course, musical works themselves do repeat throughout our lives and can become shared cultural property in the same way that styles do, and musical works can rarely be divorced from a wider concept of their stylicity. But styles develop over time to a far more significant and democratic degree, and so it's to them that socially aware composers should orientate themselves. This is not at all to say that conformity to style should be forced on composers or (re)enforced in communities – composers can repeat and differ the recurring specifics of style as they choose, and new composers will bring difference and dequantisation to styles as part of the constant generation of new images of music that stylicity brings about.

Style has been increasingly appreciated as a category of musical object in itself in recent decades, and many areas of music worldwide exemplify a new paradigm of style and work having a more equal overall focus in music-making. The international dance music of the last thirty years is a good example of this. Dance also allows communities of people to meet and celebrate the musical style of their choice together through active physical participation and has thrown up dozens of fascinating varieties of styles and sub-styles during the course of its evolution, many of which have been given names. In many cases in dance, style isn't so primary that the individuality and difference brought by composers and their works has little significance, while composers and their works aren't so primary that the recurring specifics of style become incoherent.

How and whether this balance is perceived and achieved is all relative to affordance, of course, and can be debated endlessly. Styles can have different 'sizes' – they can represent very little amounts of changing information between performances (certain types of popular music in the nineteen-twenties and -thirties, for example) or enormous amounts (say, the entirety of Western classical or rock music), and exactly at what size a style's coherency and meaning is best afforded will depend on listeners, on context and on images of music. What to me epitomises the appropriate proportions of repetition and difference within style will no doubt seem either incoherently heterogeneous or, to others at the opposite extreme, maddeningly predictable. But the point remains that the cohering effect of the recurring specifics of style, whatever 'size' that style might be, should not be forgotten or underestimated by composers.

None of this is to say that composers ought to limit all their efforts to a single, small stylistic area any more than previous generations of composers did. On the contrary – composers can switch styles dramatically or even suddenly over time, from one complex set of recurring specifics to another, and another, with a certain amount of musical works composed in each style so as to establish their specific patterns and develop them critically. Electronic music technology can both heighten the difference this process can engender and make it much easier to achieve. In fact, if composers did this they'd be revealing vast amounts of music space to their listeners as they explored a variety of styles, and refreshing their own and their listeners' imaginations because of it. Many composers do this already. It exemplifies the principle of dequantising, requantising and dequantising again, and I hope it's something we'll see a lot more of in the future.

Having noted the importance of repetition and difference – and the recurring specifics of style in particular – to the establishment of new music, let's now consider the different extents to which composers (with a certain amount of open-mindedness on the part of listeners) might go about producing new music. We can imagine new music in terms of three successive but continuous categories, each positioned progressively further along a line escaping the relative gravity of present-day convention (i.e. repetition) and heading towards ever newer and more different music and ultimately the entirety of music space. These categories are *synthesis*, *alien styles* and *alien genres*.

Synthesis: Between Earth and Elsewhere
From the apparent paradox of repetition and difference amounting to the same process, a further paradox ensues. The generation of images of music has both a positive and negative effect on new music. On the one hand, the repetition of images of music coheres music, allowing us to perceive order, enhancing affordance and meaning, and facilitating collective appreciation. On the other hand, the repetition of images of music hardens and (re)enforces music, preventing us from perceiving difference, novelty, new meanings – it constrains and deadens how we imagine music space. Repeating images of music can be said to

simultaneously create music and stifle its creativity. Music needs its images in order to live at all, but images will extinguish its vitality.

Whether or not a given amount of musical change, say, with hundreds of degrees of freedom differing to different extents, has this (re)enforcing effect on average or whether the difference is significant enough to be called 'new' overall is entirely relative, depending on the listener's affordance of the difference. There's no absolute way to tell whether musical change is new or old on average; all we can say is that the whole or parts of it are 'more' or 'less' new and differentiated, or 'more' or 'less' old and (re)enforced. The nearest we could come to knowing 'objectively' whether it was new or old would be an exhaustive statistical survey taking in musical works and listeners' reactions to them, and even that would at some point have to limit the amount of information it could constitute and remain an approximation.

However, composers can make the most of the beneficial effects of repetition while simultaneously minimising their detrimental effects by balancing repetition and difference in equal proportion, *achieving some overall equilibrium between repetition and difference* in their music. Echoing the paradox that necessitates it, we can call this equilibrium *synthesis*: it creates a synthesis of the old and the new, of the familiar and the unfamiliar, of order and disorder, of our experience and our imaginations. Synthesis *makes* the old new, the familiar unfamiliar, the ordered disordered and our lives a starting point for imagination rather than routine. Synthesis is the minimum composers can do to reveal music space and create a truly new music while still speaking a language that their listeners will understand. This language will only be partly familiar, though, because it will have changed to accommodate the difference of new grammars, new words, new meanings and new concepts, but it will have maximum effect in communicating this new information coherently if the composers are careful enough. We can liken the effect of synthesis on composers and listeners to that of being part way *between Earth and elsewhere*. Synthesis is the heady feeling of gravity falling away, leaving us suspended just outside of known or knowable images, halfway between the familiar orders of home and Heaven, Hell or an entirely new and different Earth.

Achieving synthesis is a fine balance, a tight-rope act that can be performed at ever-higher altitudes. The higher up a tight-rope walker performs, the more dangerous it gets and the more skilled s/he has to be. Similarly, the further composers reach into the unfamiliarity of a new world, the more skilfully they must accommodate the familiar in order to achieve a balance that becomes more and more precarious. A clever synthesis of old and new, or of order and disorder, is arguably a perennial hallmark of great art and music, even outside of eras where the generation of new or modern images becomes a differentiated cause in itself (as in twentieth-century modernism, for example).

The richness of synthesis is that there are so many directions in which to head away from the same-old and towards the different. The possibilities are as infinite as there are degrees of freedom in music. The equilibrium that synthesis accomplishes between repetition and difference isn't simply a fifty-fifty compromise between the old and the new, but can be achieved in so many ways and proportions, and between so many possible variables that the exact balance couldn't be precisely calculated, even if it can be felt by listeners. A small number of significant constrained variables (i.e. more differentiated images) may differ while a large number of less significant constrained variables (i.e. less differentiated images) may remain the same, or vice versa. Wholly unexpected musical objects may enter the fray, given a meaningful context by the simultaneous perception of more familiar images of musical objects. The best composers of synthesis find a way to lead listeners (and themselves) by the hand to more and more unearthly places without losing their grip, while balancing ever-larger amounts of changing information and progressively modifying certain images of musical objects until they become images of something *else*.

Synthesis could mean a balance between new pitches and old rhythms, new rhythms and old pitches, new timbres and tempos and old styles and volumes, new styles and volumes and old timbres and tempos, old durations, slightly older harmonies, slightly newer melodies and new musical objects that haven't been named or invented yet, and so on ad infinitum. It can be achieved at any level of music-making, from a few seconds of music or a single chord through the layers of musical works and styles to entire musical cultures, and may not just be a synthesis of repeating and differing sonic information but of complex non-sonic meanings too.

Particularly successful examples of synthesis include the dub style in reggae, the invention of the electric guitar and Beethoven's late works. Each of these musical objects took something old and made it new and otherworldly, taking it and its listeners to the very brink of disorder and anarchy but leaving it there, still intact and remaining highly meaningful for it. Dub moved reggae songs to the mixing desk, adjusting their textures and adding strange new reverb and delay effects, but leaving the reggae's ingredients intact enough for the whole outcome to afford a special unearthly significance. The electric guitar augmented the timbral capabilities of the classical guitar and increased its volume, opening up new worlds of musical energy that are still being explored fifty years on. The late Beethoven's unconventional approach to the form, dynamics, melody and harmony he inherited from the highly structured Viennese classical style revealed the expansive and highly emotive possibilities of musical language to a listenership that had previously favoured a more straightforward aesthetic of musical beauty.

Naturally, the perception of successful synthesis is relative and will depend on affordance. Many listeners at the time found dub, the electric guitar and Beethoven's late work to be meaningless, disorderly, irredeemably bizarre and even dangerous (in fact it was decades before the electric guitar was considered mainstream and the achievement of Beethoven's late works was generally accepted only after a century – prior to that many listeners still thought of them as the nonsensical ravings of a deaf old man). But in time dub, the electric guitar and late Beethoven proved fertile ground for the birth of electronic dance music, rock music and much nineteenth-century German classical music respectively, and all three have taken on a deep cultural and human significance that looks set to be recognised for many years to come. Synthesis may be widely effective at the time, or it may only apply for certain people at a certain time and place. It can aim to guide the largest number of people possible a small distance away from Earth, or a small amount of people a large distance towards an elsewhere, or attempt to have it both ways (which is, unsurprisingly, the most difficult to achieve). Again, this doesn't mean that synthesis is too much of a relative or slippery category to have any significance for composers and listeners alike.

Alien Styles

If all synthesis is relative, then as a category it can't be separated from new musics with any degree of novelty at all, however extreme, and may take its listeners as far into the elsewhere as it can. The further synthesis travels towards the new, however, the less easily it accommodates the familiar. This doesn't mean that composers shouldn't deliberately journey beyond the safety of synthesis, beyond the grip of Earth and into deep music space in search of new and alien musical worlds. We can call an *alien style* any music that discovers and settles on a world that's not only very different to any earthly style, but full of specifically weird and wonderful details too. With an alien style we encounter strange new musical objects that repeat and differ across unexpected dimensionalities, images we may think we come to recognise suddenly dequantise, ranges of values never lie still in the ways we're used to, complex new variables appear oddly significant and there seems to be very little order at first listen. This sort of experience can be just as fascinating to the open-minded listener as music that never strays too far from Earth.

Practically everything about an alien style seems new and unfamiliar, and yet it has a complexity of specification and richness of information potential that rivals or beats that of any more traditional earthly musical style. After a while, however, patterns begin to emerge, surreal new images come into focus and we can begin to differentiate the apparently disorderly surface of the music and learn its logics. This is because however alien it might get, an alien style is still characterised by its recurring specifics. Coming to know and differentiate these specifics until they become familiar is the journey the listener takes. Alien styles may only repeat their specifics rarely across huge lengths of time or space, their rates of difference and infor-mation-change may be very rapid, but an alien style never ultimately spurns the cohering effect of repetition or it would have no affordable gravitational pull at all.

Why must alien styles anchor themselves with the recurring specifics of style? Alien music that constantly renews its alien-ness would never allow sufficient time for images of music to be afforded and so will merely be alienating. Rather than staying in place for us to scrutinise and familiarise ourselves with its logics, it would constantly wriggle away. The final resting place for such an ethic of composition is white noise, and even if we could hear the pitches and rhythms of white noise, its unpredictability and lack of repetition would never capture a significant amount of our interest. The recurring specifics of style is a deeply relative concept and isn't a compromise so much as a lifeline, one that allows us to explore thoroughly the largest area of music space and establish life in the places we find. Composers of alien styles invent radically new musical ecosystems full of new musical objects that they re-deploy and may even evolve with each new work in the style, but that will allow listeners to put down roots. So an alien style is still a synthesis of repetition and difference, but it's one that starts from scratch, rather than repeating some aspect of prior and familiar music.

Listening to an alien style is like being a Westerner and learning a language that doesn't have an Indo-European root, like Swahili, Japanese or Cherokee, or even one that was artificially constructed with the deliberate aim of being unusual, such as Loglan, Ro or Klingon, which appropriately enough is an extraterrestrial language invented for science fiction. Learning such a language radically reveals the wider possibilities of linguistics, and so it is with music. Of course, like languages, alien styles are relative. If you speak Swahili and not English, then English would be the remote, 'alien' language. Alien styles are only alien relative to what we'd previously held to be familiar; they're afforded dependently on the listeners' experience and capacities and aren't universally distinguishable.

The image of genuinely new music many people hold is that it'll arrive as an alien style, but deliberately alien styles have been disappointingly rare in the West to date. This is largely because to be truly alien they require the creation new timbres, the technology for which has until recently been relatively difficult to muster. Some of the work of Harry Partch, early electronic music such as *Kontakte* by Stockhausen, some areas of noise music or the work of late twentieth-century electronic composers like Curtis Roads could be likened to alien styles, but not many in the age of the personal computer or synthesiser have risen to prominence. The more experimental areas of recent rock, jazz, folk and dance-derived music have often approached alien styles, but have usually retained a certain traditional foundation or haven't recurred their specifics to the point where a new stylicity applies. There are however a number of non-Western musical traditions that may *appear* 'alien' to those exclusively familiar with Western music (and conversely, Western music might seem alien to the practitioners of these musics). Many of these styles are collected on the Voyager Golden Record, of which Japanese Gagaku music, Indonesian Gamelan music and central African 'pygmy' polyphony offer particularly rich examples of detailed styles that reward close study. That such styles, so different to those of the Western tradition, have become established and successful in their respective cultures should be a source of encouragement to prospective composers of alien styles, as it shows how very far Western music is from being the necessary model of human music-making.

There are an uncountable number of complex alien styles that await discovery, and once established each could develop into such rich and different musical traditions as are represented on the Voyager Golden Record. But alien styles are only made socially successful through the increasing willingness of modern listeners to be open-minded and to listen critically, and through those who can point out and educate others as to the specifics and appeals of these styles, making them perceptible, differentiable and appreciable. But once an alien style becomes too rigid, predictable and (re)enforced, too mired in images of itself, it then becomes the new planet Earth, and thus a limitation. At that point it's time for composers and listeners to reach escape velocity and develop new images of music space once more.

Alien Genres

As we head further and further away from the familiar orders of earthly convention, we can better recognise how tiny and specific its possibilities and habits really are against the vast backdrop of a music space full of worlds on which life could be or already is established. Eventually we reach the edges of music space itself. At these outer reaches we begin to notice those ever more large-scale and fundamental recurring structures underlying our music-making habits and that situate musical activity within our lives in surprisingly specific and limited ways. To become truly alien, then, an alien style must also manifest through an *alien genre*: an entirely new way of practicing music.

Alien genres make radical departures from the norms of musical activity in Western or even wider human culture as it has existed to date. This word 'genre' has a number of different connotations in music. It's often taken to refer to a locus of musical variability that's broader than that normally meant by the word 'style'. A genre is a deeper, bigger branch in a tree of musical diversity than a style. 'Bebop' and 'early punk' may be styles, but 'jazz' and 'rock' are closer to being the 'genres' of which they belong. Similarly, the indefinite article 'a music' and its plural 'musics' has recently gained currency, and tends to imply the category of style on the much deeper level of cultural tradition. In the terminology of classical music, 'genre' is often the name given to a particular instrumental or structural form: Mozart's music is always in relatively the same Viennese classical style, but it manifested in the different genres of symphony, opera, string quartet, sacred music, keyboard (e.g. sonata) and concerto. However, in the language of music criticism (particularly that of popular music), the words 'genre' and 'style' are practically interchangeable, with the former being generally preferred and applied to styles that are even quite small and specific.

Here I follow this tendency of the word 'genre' to indicate ever broader categories of stylicity, but reach a more fundamental meaning still: a whole form of or approach to music-making. An alien genre, then, is a form of music-making typically different to the one that's been mostly practiced in the West for centuries, whose dominance has only rarely and relatively recently been challenged. An alien style is only so alien if it manifests through the traditional channels, such as being released on CD or mp3, or performed at a concert. To become an alien genre, it would have to enter and develop within our lives in an entirely different manner than that of its consumption by relatively passive listeners, which is by far the most common mode of music-making in the West at this time.

This is because alien genres lie at the very edges – or completely outside – of the images we hold of music-itself. They blur or completely erase the lines we conventionally use to divide the activity of music-making into 'composing', 'performing' and 'listening' or to confine it to certain places and occasions. We could call this currently dominant form of Western music-making *listening music*. It might seem absurd to imagine that there's any other form that music can take other than 'listening music', and even listening music is an enormous category taking in any and every way we might listen to music, from attending a concert to listening to an mp3 player, and to listening to 'muzak' over a telephone when on hold. And sound is the primary component of music, after all. But there are other musical activities too, in which the listening component isn't all there is, and which are equally an important part of music as an activity or event: composing, performing, dancing and selecting music to perform being four of the most notable (all of these would be called composing under our broader definition). We see that listening music is just a subcategory of *doing music*, or as Christopher Small called it, 'musicking' – engaging in the activity of music. 'Doing music' is music space itself, of course.

The activity that makes up an alien musical genre may not be reducible to merely listening. If listening to an alien style is like learning a remote language, experiencing an alien genre is, within the same analogy, like learning to sing, dance, paint, sculpt or play a sport – it becomes an entirely different (yet equally appreciable) activity with its own rules and systems of meaning. If we can liken musical styles to biological orders such as species, genera or families, this concept of genres in the sense I use here are closer to the root of the tree of life: entire biological kingdoms, as different to each other as an animal is from a plant, fungus or bacterium.[45] Each of these kingdoms represents a radically different way to be alive.

So what might these radically different ways of doing music be? They may not be easy to imagine as musical activity as we know it at first, but they'd be unlikely to make a major departure from the other sorts of activity, technologically-aided or otherwise, that we may engage in during our lives. Some of these activities may even conventionally be regarded as artistic. Sound art is the name sometimes given to the recent phenomenon of experiencing sound in a similar way to how we experience traditional non-sonic art. As such, sound art is often exhibited in adapted galleries or public spaces where listeners enter and leave at their discretion and may not hear the entirety of a sonic performance. The 'performance' may not even be a concrete work that has a beginning, an ending, and remains the same in between those two points.

Sound art goes some way to dethroning the concept of the 'musical work', although at a broader level it's often presented as an 'art work' in the conventional sense. The distinction many people make between the respective domains of music and sound art is disappointing, but understandable. The Western images of music-itself and of 'non-musical' art are too mutually exclusive, too deep-seated and thus too territorial for some to imagine them becoming dequantised and continuous. They're differentiable categories, but are nonetheless continuous with each other and can't be separated, whatever name we happen to give the whole. Nor should we try to separate them – the experiences afforded by sound art are those of alien musical genres.

Similarly, if music is defined as art relating primarily to sound, then it could be argued that the spoken word is music, whether live or on a recording. Our conventional understanding of music would make speech an alien musical genre. The fact that we don't tend to perceive the unaccompanied spoken word as musical activity in itself says a lot about the specific cultural way that we differentiate music and language as systems of meaning. Supposedly on the one hand we have language, with its functionality and apparently close correspondence with objects and concepts in the world, while on the other we have music, which by comparison is 'abstract', 'meaningless', more of an indulgence than a purposeful, functional inter-personal activity. Thus listening to a language we're less familiar with seems like a more 'musical' experience than listening to one we know, where we're able to attend to meanings and not just the sounds.

But the two categories are not so separable – they meet and blur together along a continuum of more and less specified meanings. Music is continuous with language, with the latter having clearer and more fixed meanings than the former. We could say that language is more *denotive*, it tends towards denoting meanings, while music is more *connotative*, tending towards connotations, but even this is arguably too reductive and differentiated to adequately express their relationship and respective capabilities. Language is often less fixed in meaning than we suppose, while the meanings of instrumental music are often more specific than we believe they can be. An alien musical genre, then, could challenge this status of music or of language by mixing the two – not in the conventional sense of adding words to music or vice versa, but in the amalgamation of music and language along the path of a single continuous variable.

Related to language is writing and its counterpart, musical notation. *Reading music* rather than listening to it could be considered an alien genre. This could mean reading anew *whilst* performing or 'sight-reading', which is a common activity seen (unnecessarily) as artistically subordinate to formal, professional performances. Or it could be reading without making a sound at all, which has been known as an appreciable aesthetic experience. If music relates primarily to sound, there's no reason why that sound can't be absent yet implied. Graphic notation, a form of musical notation that incorporates pictures, often tends towards this form of music-making. Composer Cornelius Cardew's work *Treatise* is known as a visually appealing graphic score more famously than the musical performances it may give rise to. There are no rules as to how the graphics of *Treatise* are to be translated into a musical performance, and in fact the work is equally captivating without a single sound being made. This still counts as 'art relating primarily to the production of sound,' it's just that that sound isn't actually made. It's the implication of musical performance as an abstract ideal and its problematic relationship to written instruction that gives rise to an experience that is undeniably musical, and uniquely so.

In fact any kind of musical re-interpretation along the lines of reading can be thought of as an alien genre. If reading or listening to music is a way of deriving and arranging musical information, then (re)deriving and (re)arranging can easily become a musical activity in its own right. The 'remixing' of concrete music is common in dance music and can be seen as a musical activity in itself, although we normally only consider it to be just a means to the supposedly higher cultural end of concrete listening music. Similarly music criticism and musical analysis can be thought of as alien genres of musical activity, also considered subordinate to listening music. Some forms of musical analysis even use music to interpret music: in the nineteen-fifties and -sixties the musician and music writer Hans Keller developed a form of musical analysis he called 'wordless functional analysis' and described as 'music about music'. A particularly pronounced example of music-as-music-criticism, he used it to posit the unifying structure underlying certain works of classical music without resorting to diagrams of verbal commentary. The analyses are played or listened to as musical performances, often alongside the original works. Such alien genres reveal the bizarre ways in which reading or (re)composing music can be continuous with merely listening to it more passively.

One of the areas in which alien genres would come into their own would be non-sonic variables, which are 'outside of' the conventional Western image of music-itself. This *non-sonically specific music* (not to be confused with 'sonically unspecific' music, which would simply be flexible music) could entail musical activity in some way deliberately contingent on location, time or any other constrained variables in the wider system of life. Since music is not just a passively experienced object but something actively derived from life – an active experiencing, a way of listening – then non-sonic variables could be deliberately and meaningfully incorporated into musical appreciation inseparably from the wider experiences of life. Portable music equipment such as instruments or mp3 players allow 'the same' musical works or objects to be performed in different times and places or otherwise differed across non-sonic variables and thus their images can be made new and appreciable in fresh ways. Reflecting this, 'site specific' or 'installation' art and music has recently appeared – concrete music intended to be played in certain locations, for example – although non-sonically specific music could be flexible too.

Many of the musical genres we could call 'alien' already exist, then, but are perceived to be art forms differentiated from or subordinate to listening music, and are accordingly under-explored. There are still more alien genres, however, that we might not even conventionally consider to be artistic. Some of these would be *interactive* in nature. There are many gallery art works with an interactive component, but interactive games, electronic or not, are normally culturally differentiated from 'art' in the West at the present time. Perhaps part of the reason for this is that we assume that 'art' is created by specially qualified individuals, rather than a group of relatively anonymous people, and intended for presentation in a special artistic space. But however they're created or presented, interactive music would challenge the traditional dichotomy of composer/performer and listener. These interactive musical games could be played by individuals as in solitaire or one-player video games, or by pairs or groups of people as in chess or football. They could incorporate instrument-like equipment – electric or non-electric, a complicated set of tools or a few props – or require nothing other than a human body's sound making ability. There may be a competitive element involved as participants out-do one another individually or in teams (as in rap battles, for example), or all participates could work towards a common musical goal (such as some form of unanimity, achieved, for example, at high rhythmic speeds). Non-sonic and social factors could enhance the experience of interactive music. Besides which, we often assume that games are simple, relatively unsophisticated affairs, but there's no reason why interactive music can't be as complex, specified and rich in information potential as a traditional musical performance, or even more so.

With Western music increasingly becoming orientated toward concrete musical objects (even if the musical medium isn't literally concrete, lots of composers still behave as if it is by assuming little or no autonomy on the part of any performers), many alien genres would be forms of flexible music. Interactive music is flexible music – the two terms are largely synonymous, since flexibility in music is often enabled by the mediation of performers and other figures – and the emergence of new and complex flexibilities for music-making is long overdue. It's not difficult to imagine, for example, a discrete electronic music file performed by a specially adapted device that retains broadly the same locus of variability but differs in subtle or even dramatic ways with each new performance, that is, each time we press play. Perhaps it would vary randomly, according to some underlying logic or in response to certain inputs, resulting in a flexibility not unlike that of live music. Perhaps a new explosion of flexible music will take place after a time of concreteness being the norm has become too stifling – whether or not this flexible music will be live music in the familiar sense may be irrelevant, as long as the fact of the musical objects changing at the point of performance is appreciated. Living with a flexible musical work would be less like living with a fixed and unchanging painting and more like living with a pet or a person in that they'll do slightly different things each time you encounter them but remain within broadly the same locus of variability.

One thing standing in the way of such a shift to flexibility for its own sake is the prevailing image of music-itself as amounting to a consumable product with each product having certain familiarly fixed characteristics, and concrete music has been highly amenable to this form of music-making. These products are marketed for and consumed by individuals to be listened to on headphones as they walk the streets or on domestic systems to provide a background for other activities. But this is just a latest, technologically manifested symptom of a deeper historical trend that sees musical activity differentiated into the tiny, professional elite who carry out the composition and highly specified performance and the large, silenced majority who do nothing but choose to listen to them, and pay for that privilege. This image of music-itself is responsible for the all-too-common assumption that producing music, rather than just listening to it, is the exclusive preserve of a specially talented few, and that the most valuable kind of music-making is that which is left to the professionals.

But there are many ways of enjoying music that lie outside of this passive, solipsistic model, and many non-Western or pre-industrial cultures know (or knew) this. Disappointingly, it's collective, socially equal music – music flexibly and equally created during its performance by a society of people – that's becoming the alien genre in the West. Our ability to imagine such a form of music-making, particularly as successful or appealing, is fading fast. Overturning this dominant image of music-itself and returning the capacity of music-making to everyone in the general public, along with a new aesthetics of social, collective music-making to rival that of personal listening, must be one of the majors goals for the future of music. At stake is nothing less than our ability to imagine new and more democratic ways of living through music's capacity to represent them.

The musical objects operating within alien genres needn't be those of alien styles, though they can be. A synthesis of repetition and difference, of familiar and unfamiliar forms, could still be achieved through an alien genre. In fact, finding some way of accommodating the familiar would be a perfect way to introduce people to a new form of music-making. Even if it may be difficult to imagine it happening, alien genres such as interactive or collective music can develop from the isolated, simplistic or unrecognised experiments they are today. They can – given time and effort – become whole art forms with long repertoires every bit as rich and culturally significant as those that have already evolved into complex systems of meaning over centuries, of which the listening music we know is just one. Alien genres are closer to the multifarious experiences and activities of life as a whole than any other more limited image of music-itself. More than any other class of musical objects, they recognise the mutually inclusive and mutually supportive relationship between music and everything we do in our wider lives.

New Instruments

The three tiers of new music described here can all be taken as implying that composers ought to be sophisticated engineers, keeping every possible musical variable in their sights and ready in their toolkits. Carefully balancing the old and the new or designing wholly new styles or genres of music may be effective ways of expanding listeners' imaginations, but when it comes to using the necessary technology it's hardly an easy undertaking, at least at the current time of writing. With much music technology currently so complex, advanced and inaccessible that simply owning some and being able to use it effectively can be the basis of a professional career, not all would-be composers have the time or resources to acquire and master the equipment that could help them create new musical systems completely from scratch. Of course, a great many alien styles or genres may not need the very best and latest music software and hardware to be performed, but those who are able to master the technology have often provided the spur for new music-making in the form of *new instruments*.

Instrument-building is one of the oldest alien genres to make up musical activity, and again, it's one that's traditionally thought of as aesthetically differentiated from and subordinate to listening music. But to build an instrument is to create a musical object and thus to compose music. The difference between conventional composition and instrument-building is merely the latter's greater degree of flexibility, and how that allows further composers and performers to use those instruments in more specific ways. It's too easy to assume that instrument-building is a thing of the past and that the limitations represented by specific instruments have been superseded by the virtually infinite electronic possibilities of Cage's sound space and its technological successors. While this is true, the fact remains that few composers have mastered the modern digital audio workstation to the point where they have (or realise that they have) an enormity of music space at their fingertips. Still fewer people have the ability or inclination to build new software or hardware instruments and a minority of them would conventionally use the word 'composer' to describe themselves if they didn't also make a concerted effort to produce their own original music (and even then, they may well have used the term 'producer').

But since it's not music space's breadth of musical possibility and difference in itself but the affordability enabled by the recurring specifics of repetition that will make new and modern music viable in the post-experimental age, the importance of musical instruments as specifically constrained loci of variability is greater than ever. Where they cannot master the entirety of music space, composers will, unknowingly perhaps, rely heavily on the creation of instruments built by those with the power to do so. These instruments may bring composers and listeners to radically new areas of music space, but they'll need to be as intuitive to use as any more traditional musical instrument. The history of music shows that well-designed, accessible and even bizarre new instruments will quickly and successfully be picked up and incorporated into new musical styles, even by untrained musicians in economically impoverished communities – jazz (which incorporated the saxophone and drum kit), electric blues (the electric guitar), hip hop (the sampler), house and techno (synthesisers and drum machines) being cases in point. Most recently, the contemporary equivalent of these instruments – relatively basic software run from a relatively basic laptop computer – has proved successful in galvanising musical innovation among young and untrained composers, becoming advantageous to styles such as grime and UK funky in London and similar dance music throughout the world.

These trends look set to continue, but it's up to the instrument-builders to make sure that exotic new sounds are easily accessible to these new-music-hungry communities of would-be composers. Some of these exotic sounds may be complex and incorporate advanced sonic engineering to create new forms of sound synthesis, or they may simply make less established forms of synthesis more intuitive and accessible. Granular synthesis (which splits a sound into 'grains' of certain minute durations and rearranges them) and fast Fourier transforms (which split a sound into its constituent pitches and can rearrange them) are two forms of sound synthesis that have to date been the exclusive preserve of advanced electronic composers, and they only occasionally appear in underground popular music. They're also very demanding of computing power, but as processor speeds increase there's no reason why advanced granular synthesis or fast Fourier transforms can't produce spectacular sonic effects through the humble laptop or some modest piece of hardware.

In order for this to happen, though, instrument-builders must be able to present this technology to the public intuitively and accessibly. This may well mean constraining the full possibilities of the technology to certain presets (as many widely-used synthesisers do) or 'black boxing' (not revealing the precise workings and methods of the system) but whatever its constraints, a well-designed instrument will quickly find its audience. As they exist now, largely in obscure or prohibitively technical software or equipment, granular synthesis and fast Fourier transforms will never find the wide audience they deserve.

On the other hand, some forms of synthesis have been available for decades, but their capabilities haven't been nearly as fully exploited as they could be. Sample-based synthesis, which uses an inputted sample as the starting-point for sound synthesis, has been used in largely very basic ways since the nineteen-eighties, but its capacity to create strange and complex waveforms (whether or not the original sample is recognisable as a certain recorded sound in the end) remains under-explored. This becomes particularly urgent in light of the return to basic waveform synthesis seen in the last decade, which generally has a recognisably 'electro' sound. While electro timbres are a rich musical resource comparable to the primary colours of visual art, their use does currently (re)enforce a long-held cultural image of electronic music as artificial and robotic, whereas complex waveforms such as those enabled by sample-based synthesis have very broad and organic timbral possibilities. These capacities will only be accessible if instrument-builders can bring them to the attentions of composers in a straightforward way.

There are even certain images of the variabilities instruments have (images of 'instrumentality') that music technologists can challenge. Doing so would create what we could call an *alien instrument*. Although it no longer is today, the synthesiser was an alien instrument in the nineteen-seventies because it could vary its timbre so much more radically than any other previously invented instrument could. Alien instruments would have unusual loci of musical control. They may quantise, dequantise or requantise musical variables in unconventional, innovative ways. They may provoke focussed experimentation by limiting ranges of values that are much greater on more traditional instruments. They may even allow traditional variables to be manipulated in new or physically different ways. The Kaoss Pad is one such instrument, which uses an intuitive touchscreen display to allow its user to control a number of more conventional effects.

The power of a single instrument is in its constraining of music space and how that encourages specificity, not in its capacity to access enormous areas of it within itself. For many composers, the infinite possibilities of musical software that can do anything (but only if you can engineer it) are little more than paralysing, often causing them to retreat into familiar musical systems. Having said this, it's possible to imagine instrument-building as a form of the new music category of synthesis described earlier, with the balance achieved being that of amount of music space accessed versus an ability to make that access easy and effortless. Along these lines, a music software programme through which music space's virtually infinite possibilities are made as easy and inspiring to explore as a piano or a simple video game – that makes travelling through music space highly psychologically 'affordable' – is the ultimate goal of the music technology, and would heavily reward both composers and listeners alike.

Such a programme would be able to create and represent any amount of basic or 'built up' structures of musical variables for the purposes of both flexible and concrete composition and play them as a live performance in real time, moving quickly from basic to higher structures using a visual display that zooms through all scales of music-making at the touch of a display or the drag of a finger. It would allow composers of any background whatsoever to create complex alien styles (or even perhaps alien genres) without difficulty and in minutes, if so desired. What's more, the programme would be free and easy to access, and could be run from increasingly ubiquitous portable touchscreen computers. It's not difficult to imagine, far enough into the future, a world in which such devices are more common than mobile phones – their ancestors – are today. Perhaps they'd even be as commonplace, inexpensive and recyclable as sheets of paper (which they may well closely resemble). They may not be privately owned to the extent that phones and laptops are today – if everyone's files were stored online and accessible with passwords or biometric data, devices for accessing, processing and creating personal or public information could be inter-changeable, passing from person to person like free newspapers do on public transport. They may even be supplied to people free of charge by the state, funded by taxes, with access to them considered a human right just as clean drinking water is.[46] And again, far enough into the future, such devices could be freely accessible to anyone in any of the world's cultures, rather than just a paying Western elite as they are today.[47]

Run on these devices, an intuitive and extensive music-making programme as described above would finally level the musical playing field, presenting the full potential of Cage's sound space to anyone and everyone, whatever their background. Its creation would present a formidable challenge to software designers and the end result could be achieved in any number of ways. In fact, there may not be one single programme but a range of coexisting programmes, each with different strengths and weaknesses, different trade-offs between capability and ease of use. But I think it's highly probable that programmes like this will enter use, most likely slowly, developing over the course of many decades, at some point this century. When they do, and when they become universally accessible, the most important revolution in the history of music – that of human culture's total access to music space – will be complete.

Epilogue: Into the Future

In Part 2 I referred to the music-technological empowerment of the general public as a revolution. It enables the shift of power in musical production and innovation from the few to the many. Accordingly, the locus of that innovation shifts from the lesser to the greater and ultimately to the infinite. This has been one of the most exciting developments in musical culture in the last thirty years, and the resulting accomplishments of musicians not trained or working in traditional professional circles have been growing steadily in significance. These people, and ultimately all of us, are the composers of the twenty-first century. Many of them have already taken small steps towards establishing a new image of musical modernity.

The ideas in this book were in part provoked by the concrete music composed in and around Western electronic dance music, and the ongoing debates over its aesthetics. Electronic dance music is a scene that's been nurturing the style-based exploration of modern music spaces in all their detailed potential for over twenty-five years, and has in many respects begun to replace Western classical music and jazz as the music of choice for young composers and intellectuals in recent decades. As such, it has become the site of a new musical avant-garde, one not necessarily resembling those of previous generations. Its innovation is built upon repetition and the recurring specifics of style, which respond with varying degrees of loyalty to the traditional requirements of the dancefloor.

In particular, the music released under the name Burial in the last decade has stood out from this energetically fertile milieu as an achievement of particular importance. It suggests the dancefloor but, like many artists of the last twenty years who borrow some stylistic specifics from dance music, it reaches a level of subtlety and sophistication that transcends rave functionality and rewards close, thoughtful listening. It can be listened to as deeply hauntological in that it incorporates vinyl crackle and highly evocative, melancholy echoes of the previous decade of rave music, expressing the nostalgia and dilapidation of nocturnal London in the early twenty-first century. The music is also forward-looking, however, in that it represents an example of someone with no particular musical training establishing their own original, idiosyncratic stylistic language – one that nonetheless manages to communicate immediate, clear and very specific meanings to listeners. In effortlessly combining these two directions, Burial's work presents a complex, imaginative and deeply instructive example of the synthesis concept from Part 3 as it can be applied today.

We're told that the technology Burial uses – a programme called 'Sound Forge' – is amongst the most basic anyone could use to create music. It isn't even particularly designed for musical composition and was run on an old and failing computer. Burial's software can't even do much to quantise time: many programmes typically move sounds to the nearest subdivision of the beat automatically, according to an underlying pulse. The dequantised percussion and samples we encounter in the music are no technical failure or amateurish accident, however, but one of the finest examples to date of the subtle and expressive potential in electronic music's precision continuous values. Burial also achieves startling results with electronic effects like stereo and reverb and handles all the musical variabilities afforded by even the simplest electronic music software with a complexity and sophistication that seemed previously unimaginable. Perhaps Burial is the archetypal twenty-first century modern composer, an early sign of things to come.[48]

In the last few years, dequantised electronic dance music (much of it apparently inspired by Burial and the label he releases on, Hyperdub) has hinted at a new musical world. Not only are the possibilities of dequantised time being thoroughly explored as a style in itself, resulting in both subtle and widely skewed rhythms and textures, but pitch has seen some dequantisation too, with detuned and synthesisers continuously 'gliding' through pitch and timbre values, bringing alien sounds to the communal embodiment of the dance-floor. In a less literal sense, the stylistic categories that had previously differentiated the various styles of dance music have been dequantised, melted back into the broader continuity of dance music space, with mixtures of hip hop, dubstep, house and new styles highlighting bizarre musical objects spread across unusual dimensionalities, pointing to the full breadth of music space. Actress, Ikonika, Zomby and Hudson Mohawke are just four of the most significant names to have ventured into these spaces, while record labels (which are musical objects too) such as Hyperdub, Night Slugs, Numbers, Hessle Audio, Hotflush, Hemlock, Leaving Records and many others have all established a thriving, collective presence in these new territories.

This book could have been called 'Continuous Music' for a number of reasons, each of which gets to the core of the ideas presented in it. Firstly, the word relates to infinity through the notion of continuous variables, which can theoretically represent an infinite number of values. We've seen how the relatively discrete and differentiated musical objects or images of music we know can be 'dequantised' back into that infinite continuity and unified there, that they are continuous with each other, and with many other undiscovered structures 'between' them, within an infinite music space. Thus they can all be comparable and conceivably equal, seen on the same terms rather than through the traditional hierarchies. This dequantisation permits a 'bird's eye view' of musical variability, situating what we know against a backdrop of alternative possibilities. It also implies that we could dequantise even further – that music is continuous with the everyday life from which it emerges and is then differentiated, continuous with anything we might have previously considered non-music or outside of music.

This leads into a second sense of the word 'continuous' as in 'continuously' – a state of being constant or ubiquitous. Music in its entirety can be thought of as a single event that's happening all the time, even in between what we normally think of as the separate musical performances we differentiate it into. We imagined style as a musical work that transcends any number of discrete performances, spanning the much longer time periods in which they occur. Any music, in fact, can take place outside of the traditional cultural borders delineating musical performances. This isn't a new idea, of course, but the notion of dequantising images of music presented here arrives at it easily and continuously with all music-making.

The third sense of the word 'continuous' relates it to the word 'continuing', as in continuing along an unbroken line. Many people believe, for all kinds of reasons, that we live in an age in which that the spirit of new music has been discontinued, and in some respects and contexts this is a valid concern. The system of infinite variability outlined in this book doesn't break from the avant-garde traditions of a century ago, but rather extends them to the nth degree. In doing so, I hope to have suggested a way to imagine new music being composed long into the future.

A key difference today's new music has to the avant-gardes of a century ago, however, is the former's technological resources. Infinite music in its truly infinite sense relies on technology to actualise it. After all, it's much easier for a precision machine, observing continuous variables, to perform a pitch of precisely 443.25 Hz than a human being controlling a string or a mouthpiece, not to mention control reverb and unique effects like distortion. This is all relative, of course, music always has depended on technologies, whether physical, mental or social, ever since the first drums and bone-flutes. Technology, then, is a key medium for the potential actualisation of infinite music, and greatly enhances any journey towards it. But it would be too easy to overemphasise the importance of cutting-edge or future technology at the expense of present day concerns. For one thing, despite the recent spread of software technology in the West, computer access for the whole human race itself is still very much a pipedream, much less easy access to music software. The future of music starts in the present, and infinite musical possibilities are reachable today. They may draw on instruments and technologies that have existed for decades, or even much longer, that may be very basic. Even the possibilities of collective, interactive music using nothing but the human body are virtually infinite, and those possibilities are far more widely accessible in the present day than those of any computer.

This should remind us that access to the infinity of music space isn't just a matter of using the latest electronic music technologies. It's also socially and culturally barred to a disturbing and unrealised extent. For every teenager willing to try creating their own sound using intuitive musical software on a laptop, there are far more people who feel that they have insufficient musical ability, that they can't be composers and shouldn't participate in musical performance. The ideology telling us that music-making is the preserve of the specially talented or trained few is fading every year and is fast being proved very wrong by the likes of Burial, but it's still a pernicious and deeply embedded image of music-making-itself. Some people resign themselves to 'tone-deafness' (a much rarer condition than Western culture would have you believe) or its equivalents, and withdraw from musical activity. Even where tone-deafness really does apply, pitched tones are only one of music's many variables. Listening (which is composing), too, is often assumed to require some special education, and people are discouraged from trying to listen critically to find their own, new affordances. We call ourselves musically finite.

These ideologies stem from and perpetuate the capitalist perception of music as a static object to be paid for and consumed, whose qualities and appeals (i.e. its value) are left to be dictated by elite professional standards of taste, which are unsurprisingly only attainable by that same elite. Instead, we should see it as a process, a performance event that calls forth musical objects as loci of difference rather than as fixed, commodifiable entities. So it's understandable that one of the biggest objections to infinite and democratically controlled musical possibility is that it'll result in an inundation of supposedly poor-quality material, diluting and obscuring the high-quality material. The first response to this is that musical dilettantes are regularly less talentless and aesthetically helpless than we suspect, though it usually takes some imagination to see the workings of their innovative idiolects with respect to our own prior images of music. Burial and the non-professionalised, communal music-making of many non-Western cultures – most famously, those of Africa or of African descent or influence – are proof of this.

The second response is that, as we saw when looking at alien genres, the aesthetic gratification of musical activity can conceivably lie to a significant degree in the fact of taking part itself, not merely in the attainment or perception of highly specific standards of value. A good analogy here is that of football, or a number of similar sports. Many people who enjoy watching professional football on television see no problem in playing the same sport casually, with friends or family in the park or a back garden. They know they're not as good at football as the star players they appreciate on television, but they themselves play anyway because they enjoy taking part, they enjoy *playing* – whatever their level of skill – rather than merely watching. An equivalent tradition of casual participation in music-making among adolescents and adults of any class is scarce. Even where amateur musicians do perform, for audiences or for themselves, it's often felt to be in the context of reaching professional standards and success, ending in the all-important record contract, fame and the commodified concrete sound objects that follow. This is not to say that skill plays no part in casual football or casual music-making, but the levels of skill felt to be required for participation in music-making under late capitalism is prohibitively and discouragingly high.

If music is infinite, then its composers are infinite and potentially infinite in number. No restrictive idea (image) about music-making should tell us otherwise. Music can be as personal, as collective and as potentially free as any of the other activities of human life from which it's ultimately indistinguishable. No matter how far from Earth it travels, music can become just as much a part of our everyday – yet perhaps otherworldly – human lives and achievements.

Appendix: Alan Lomax's Cantometrics System

As discussed in the main part of the book, twentieth-century avant-garde composers such as the serialists and John Cage (with his 'sound space') saw music as a system described by a small number of certain variables, with a musical work amounting to one of the many permutations of the possible values of those variables. But it was not just composers who were describing music's diverse possibilities in terms of systems of variables in the nineteen-fifties and -sixties. The American scholar, writer and field worker Alan Lomax was most famous for recording thousands of folk songs from around the world and publicly promoting folk music at a time when it was rapidly disappearing. His ethnomusicological 'cantometrics' project of the nineteen-sixties, in conjunction with the Anthropology Department at Columbia University, is less well-known. As Lomax and his collaborator Victor Grauer put it, 'Cantometrics, a coined word which means a measure of song or song as a measure, is a method for systematically and holistically describing the general features of accompanied or unaccompanied song performances.'[49]

Using a rating system of thirty-seven variables given by a 'cantometric coding book', every folk song style in the world could conceivably be described by its 'cantometric profile' and thus be compared on the same terms. Hundreds of songs from over two-hundred cultures were rated in the course the project. Noting that the system's attention to the subtleties of vocal delivery improves on more conventional systems of notation, Lomax and Grauer suggested that cantometrics can 'broadly characterize song performance style in such a way that the main families of sung performances may be recognised, their geographical distribution mapped, and their relationship to cultural continuity, acculturation, and the expressive arts perceived.'[50]

As a describing system, cantometrics is a 'folk song style space' and thus a fitting counterpart to Cage's sound space, tailored to the traditional popular (i.e. produced by the people) musics of the time. And like Cage's sound space, cantometrics can also be considered as a composing system for flexible music, as a set of tools for imagining styles that do not (yet) exist. Note too that the system measures style as a category in itself, rather than individual performances or musical works.

Lomax's system wasn't just 'the establishment of a structurally and historically meaningful taxonomy of the world's folk song styles', however.[51] His aim was to find correlations between features in the cantometric profiles of song styles and the social mores of the cultures that had produced the styles. For example, one of the observations motivating the study was that 'In southern Spain, where sexual sanctions were Oriental in their stringency, a piercing, high-pitched, squeezed, narrow vocal delivery was cultivated... [and] North of the Pyrenees... where sexual sanctions were mild and contact between the sexes was easy and relaxed, there was a strong preference for well-blended choirs singing in open and low-pitched voices.'[52] Lomax's hypothesis was that:

Song style seems to summarize, in a compact way, the ranges of behaviour that are appropriate to one kind of cultural context. If style carries this load of social content, however, song can no longer be treated as a wayward, extra, belated, though pleasant afterthought upon the serious business of living. Song presents an immediate image of a culture pattern. A man's favourite tune recalls to him not only some pleasant memory, but a web of relationships that makes his life possible.[53]

While such an assumption is often still central, even fundamental, to the academic disciplines of ethnomusicology and the
sociology of music, the results of the cantometrics project were at
best inconclusive, and in the twenty-first century these disciplines rarely engage with the system in detail. Where such correlations between musical life and social life do exist, cantometrics
was both too strict and too crude to reveal their structure,
especially as universal throughout the world's populations. But
fifty years on, Lomax's statement is still very persuasive on the
topic of music as a powerful form of social (and by extension,
political) communication, continuous with 'the business of
living' and not merely a decorative 'afterthought', differentiated
from and supplementary to it.

Cantometrics remains a fascinating chapter in the history of
ethnomusicology and a key example of a detailed system of
musical variables lying outside of the historic locus of Western,
largely classical composition theory. The thirty-seven variables
(or 'lines') of the system and their values are summarised below
as a further example of the many different types of musical
variables that can be observed – be they composed or described
– in human music-making.

1. **The vocal group**. Describes the 'social structure of the singing
group', their 'degree of integration'. Values range from 'one
singer', through 'one solo singer after another', 'social unison
with a dominant leader', 'social unison with the group
dominant', simple and overlapping alternations between leaders
and choruses and finally 'interlocking' ('the group is divided
into two or more parts which are rhythmically distinct and
melodically complementary.')

2. **The relationship between the accompanying orchestra and
the vocal part**. Values range from 'a small orchestra (one to three
players), accompanying the vocal part and subordinate to it' to

'an orchestra of four or more players in complementary relationship to the singers'.

3. **The instrumental group**. Generally the same as line 1, but describing the 'social structure of the orchestra alone'.

4. **Basic musical organisation of the voice part**. Describes the texture of the singing. Values range from 'two or more singers who are totally unrelated musically' ('the effect may be similar to a mob scene'), through 'monophony', 'unison', 'heterophony' and finally 'polyphony'.

5. **Tonal blend of the vocal group**. Describes the timbral consistency among the singers. Values range from 'minimal blend' ('singers make no attempt to match one another in tone. Individual voices stand out. The effect is harsh and often noisy.') to 'maximal blend' ('the singers match each other's tone in such a way as to present the effect of a single tone quality'.)

6. **Rhythmic blend of the vocal group.** Describes the 'degree of rhythmic coordination among the singers'. Values range from 'minimal rhythmic blend' ('an extremely ragged and uncoordinated performance') to 'maximal rhythmic blend' ('precise coordination at every rhythmic level').

7. **The basic musical organisation of the orchestra**. Generally the same as line 4, but describing the orchestra.

8. **Tonal blend of the orchestra**. Generally the same as line 5, but describing the orchestra.

9. **Rhythmic blend of the orchestra**. Generally the same as line 6, but describing the orchestra.

10. **Words to nonsense.** Describes 'the proportion of the text in the whole song which seems to be repeated or that consists of "nonsense material"... [which] includes nonsense syllables, nonsense words, vocal segregates, babbling, ululating, animal imitations, shouts, cries, moans, laughter, sobbing, grunting, and the like'. Values range from 'words dominant', ('different syllables, words, and phrases, with little or no repetition or use of nonsense material') to 'the text seems to be almost entirely composed of repetition of some sort or of nonsense'.

11. **Overall vocal rhythmic scheme.** Broadly speaking, describes the meter of the singing. Values range from 'one-beat rhythm' ('a series of equally accented single notes of about the same length') through 'simple meter', 'complex meter', 'irregular meter' and finally 'parlando rubato' ('"Free rhythm" in which no regularly recurring beat can be distinguished... often close to speech in general effect'.)

12. **Rhythmic relationship within the singing group.** Values range from 'rhythmic unison' through 'complex polyrhythm' and finally 'rhythmic counterpoint'.

13. **Overall rhythmic structure of the accompaniment.** Same as line 11, but for the accompaniment.

14. **Rhythmic relationship within the accompanying group.** Same as line 12, but for the accompaniment.

15. **Melodic shape.** Values range from 'arched' through 'terraced' (a 'cascading descent' punctuated by 'periods of levelling off'), 'undulating' and finally 'descending'

16. **Melodic form.** Values range from 'canonic or round form' to 'complex litany with a high degree of variation in each section'.

17. **Phrase length**. Values range from 'a very, very long phrase' ('16 to 25+ seconds') to 'short and very short phrases' ('1-2 seconds')

18. **Number of phrases**. Values range from 'there are more than eight phrases before a full repeat' to 'one or two phrases, symmetrically arranged'.

19. **Position of the final tone**. Values range from 'the final tone is the lowest note of the song' to 'the final tone is the highest note of the song'.

20. **Range**. Describes the range of pitch. Values range from 'a monotone to a major second' (i.e. two semitones) to 'two octaves or more'.

21. **Interval width**. Describes the 'kinds of [pitch] intervals that occur in the melody'. Values range from 'monotone' to 'very wide intervals' ('intervals of a fourth or fifth or larger predominate')

22. **Polyphonic type**. Describes 'the use of simultaneously produced intervals other than the unison or octave'. Values range from 'drone polyphony' ('one or more tones are held or repeated while the melody follows its own course') through 'isolated chords', 'parallel chords', 'harmony' and finally 'counterpoint'.

23. **The degree of embellishment used by the singer(s)**. Describes 'qualification of or ornamentation upon the "basic" melodic line'. Values range from 'extreme embellishment' to 'little or no embellishment'.

24. **Tempo**. Describes the speed of the singing. Values range from 'extremely slow' to 'very fast'.

25. **Volume**. Values range from 'very soft' to 'very loud'.

26. **Rubato in the voice part**. Describes 'how strictly tempo is maintained during a performance'. Values range from 'extreme rubato' to 'no rubato' ('strict time').

27. **Rubato in the instruments**. Same as line 26, but 'applied to the accompanying instruments'.

28. **Glissando**. Describes 'the effect created when the voice slides from one tone to another, passing through all the intermediate pitch levels'. Values range from 'maximal glissando' to 'no glissando'.

29. **Melisma**. Describes the extent that 'the same syllable [is] sung (or stretched over) two or more basic notes of the melody'. Values range from 'most of the pitches are unarticulated' to 'syllabic' ('all of the pitch changes are articulated').

30. **Tremolo**. Describes the extent of 'a quavering or shaking in the voice that is heard as an undulation between two closely adjacent pitches or tone colours', which I've described earlier as 'vibrato'. Values range from 'tremolo is heavy throughout the song' to 'little or no tremolo'.

31. **Glottal shake**. Describes 'activity in the pharyngeal or glottal area' at the back of the throat: 'glottal stops, glottal trills, considerable amounts of glottal articulation, forceful glottal articulation, glottal stroke, and strongly emphasized, wide vibrato from deep in the throat.' 'Some singers actually manipulate their Adam's apple with their fingers to produce this effect.' Values range from 'strongly characterized by glottal activity' to 'little or no noticeable glottal activity'.

32. **Register**. Describes 'whether the singer is sticking to the middle of his [pitch] range, singing at the upper or lower end of it, or pushing it to one or both extremes'. Values range from 'very high' ('usually falsetto in men') to 'very low' ('the singer is probably producing his lowest tones').

33. **Vocal width**. Describes the 'scale, ranging at the extremes from a very pinched, narrow, squeezed voice to the very wide and open-throated singing tone of Swiss yodelers'. Values range from 'very narrow' through 'very wide' ('wide-open, resonant') and finally 'yodel'.

34. **Nasalization**. Describes 'nasal tone... as... produced by a speaker with a... bad cold, or as a sound produced when the soft palate drops and air is forced through the nose.' Values range from 'marked nasalization' to 'little or no nasalization'.

35. **Raspiness**. Describes 'hoarseness, harshness, grating, buzzing'. Values range from 'extreme raspiness' ('an extremely harsh, hoarse, raspy, grating voice') to 'voices which lack rasp'.

36. **Accent**. Describes 'the strength of the attack on sung tones... certain singers – American Indians, for instance – force out the first note in every small phrase with great muscular drive.' Values range from 'very forceful accent or attack' to 'very relaxed, almost unaccented rhythmic motion'.

37. **Enunciation of consonants**. Describes 'the degree of precision of enunciation of consonants as against the other extreme of the parameter – a slurring of the syllables.' Values range from 'very precise' to 'very slurred'.[54]

The variables are quantised to different numbers of possible values, with many also including a 'not applicable' option, from just three values (e.g. line twenty-nine, melisma) to thirteen (e.g. line one, the vocal group). When multiplied together, these numbers show that the cantometrics system could recognise and differentiate 1,589,200,499,250,000,000,000,000,000, roughly 1.6×10^{27}, or over one and half octillion possible folk song styles. This exceeds the number of stars in the known universe.

Acknowledgements

This book's roots go back through many years of long conversations with musicians and music lovers. Many gave crucial advice and support during its writing. Thank you to Annie McDermott, John Erde, Mark Fisher, Christopher Garrard, Tom Hyde, Athena Lill, Edwin Mak, Hannah Sander and Alex Williams in particular, and all the countless musicians and composers whose work and imaginations nurtured the ideas presented here. Mention must also go to the 'Transversal Space' set up in May 2010 by students occupying the Philosophy Department of Middlesex University in protest against its closure. While visiting I attended free lectures on Spinoza and calculus, and encountered books by Deleuze and about his work, all of which had a decisive impact on my research. Hopefully this book attests in some way to the ongoing relevance and vitality of philosophy, whose powers of imagination are set, as ever, against those who lack it.

Notes

Introduction

1 Leonard Bernstein, 'The Infinite Variety of Music' in *The Infinite Variety of Music* (1968), p. 29.

2 What would it be like to hear music and be able to say nothing more specific, to be able to pin it down to no narrower category, than that you'd heard 'music'? Not 'rock', 'classical' or 'jazz' music, not music on a flute, guitar, synthesiser or any familiar instrument, not music from a familiar work or by recognisable composers – what would that music, music without categories, sound like?

Part I: Musical Variables

3 Brian Everitt, *The Cambridge Dictionary of Statistics* (2006).

4 Roger Porkess, *Collins Dictionary of Statistics* (2004).

5 Timbre is sometimes called the 'tone colour' of a sound. Put simply, a sound's timbre depends on what kind of instrument is playing it and, beyond that, how the instrument is being played. Violins, muted trumpets and non-muted trumpets all have different timbres, for example, regardless of what pitch or volume they're being played at.

6 These variables could be called the 'parameters' of the reverb. The words 'variable' and 'parameter' tend to overlap in meaning and usage with the latter ultimately having no strictly narrow definition, especially in everyday use. More technically, the word 'parameter' is often used to describe a specific sort of variable that determines a property of a system or function that controls other variables. The sounds going into and coming out of the reverb effect are input and output variables while the 'duration of reverb' setting could be called a parameter; it has an effect on the output variable. Since both variables and parameters can be controlled by

composers at the point of music's maximum possibilities (which is what concerns us here), that is, they're both ultimately equal in their ability to vary, they can ultimately both considered *independent variables*, I won't distinguish between variables and parameters in this book. If a composer wanted to distinguish between variables and parameters, say in order to create a 'composing machine' that required the setting of parameters controlling what was produced from a variable input, the entire output of that machine would be limited in comparison to the total possibilities of music, which are virtually infinite, being only constrained in a physical sense by the parameters of the universe itself (i.e. its constants: the speed of light, Planck's Constant etc.), which composers cannot control (at the current time of writing).

7 Similarly, the specification of a cathedral for the musical work may have been made for sonic reasons (the reverb) or non-sonic reasons (religious, perhaps), or both.

8 In fact, with changes this minor, few people would probably say, if asked, that it was now 'a different musical work'. Most people would say it was a different 'version' of the same work, perhaps. This only goes to show the tenaciousness of notions of a musical work having an abstract, immortal 'essence', but it's also a natural result of the fact that composers rarely create pieces of music that are so similar to each other.

9 In turn, since the twentieth century many composers (among them John Cage, Christian Wolff and Morton Feldman) have written music that is much *less* sonically specified than conventional classical music. They write certain loose instructions and guidelines for the musical performance in the score, but leave much of the outcome to chance or the choice of the performer within the possible scope of those instructions. This music has been called 'indeterminate', 'aleatory' (for chance operations in the music), 'impro-

visatory', and 'experimental' (though less technically, 'experimental' does also tend to refer to music that is unusual in a more general sense).

10 To a certain extent, this music already exists as a sonic equivalent of installation art sometimes called 'sound installations' and in various experimental compositions. But such works could not easily be described as a coherent, popular style in its own right, with its own aesthetic tradition to rival that of traditional musics, anywhere near to the extent to which it could be. Live music doesn't really count, as we rarely consider its varying locations to be a site of primary aesthetic interest.

11 Christopher Small, *Musicking: The Meanings of Listening and Performing* (1998).

12 Actually, we could say that all variables that describe sound, even pitch, can be broken down into just two: time and the force of air acting on the ear drum, which is given as the amplitude of a sound wave. Similarly, much sound playback equipment only sees music in terms of two variables: time and voltage (which then goes on to make a membrane vibrate air, causing sound). Since it's difficult to compose detailed music using just these two variables (to say the least), composers effectively do the reverse and build these variables up into higher structures, such as pitch and volume (which depends on the variable properties of the air), and then timbre, then texture, rhythm etc.

13 In order to survive the destruction of the Earth by the Sun in approximately five to eight billion years or any eventuality with a similar effect, a performance of *Organ2/ASLSP* on pipe or electronic organ could be set up in a free-floating spacecraft and initially projected to finish at a time as close to the anticipated death of the universe as conditions make possible. In order for it to carry on sounding, the spacecraft would need to supply the organ with energy, which would

need to be obtained from a relatively renewable energy source external to the craft, such as the Sun. After the complete extinction of the Sun's light, power could come from a battery that had been charged using solar panels while the craft was close to the Sun and thereafter could come from starlight or the fusion of trace hydrogen atoms in the interstellar medium, or else the resources of other astronomical bodies. Some form of permanent onboard intelligence would probably be needed to play the piece and to locate and regulate energy and resources effectively and adaptively for the purposes of maintaining the music, the organ, the spacecraft and itself for the longest possible time. An optimum performance of Cage's piece would require some compromise between playing the notes of the piece in the correct temporal proportions and some constantly adapting estimation of what total duration of the piece looks to be physically possible, regarding the length of time the craft and/or the universe can be made to survive. Therefore, the onboard intelligence would need to be able to constantly observe the conditions of both the spacecraft and the universe, and adapt models of stellar evolution, the life of the universe, cosmological models and any threat to the craft's survival so as to assess them and react accordingly in self-preservation and so as to always play the piece according to the longest possible duration. Extrapolating from these models, it would constantly modify the projected dates and conditions of the demise of the craft and/or the universe and use these conclusions to constantly recalculate the appropriate proportions of the notes in time as the piece is played. If multiple universes exist and the spacecraft could transport itself safely from one to another so as to continue playing the piece after the death of the universe of its origin, the onboard intelligence would need to be aware of this and how to accomplish it at the earliest possible opportunity and be able to adapt and apply this knowledge at every subsequent opportunity to the playing of the music proportionally. This is how *Organ2/ASLSP* could be played for as long as was ultimately possible, if technology (and the earthly resources to begin the project) permitted, though such a performance wouldn't quite be in keeping with the more playfully philosophical spirit of the piece.

14 There are a number of ways in which the phrase 'music with moving parts' could be misunderstood, the main being that the various 'parts' within the music (i.e. the number of voices within it) display movement. This, incidentally, would simply be a problematic definition of polyphonic music. The parts in polyphonic music don't literally move, just as the same object depicted in different places in different frames on a video or cinema screen doesn't literally move. Any movement experienced by listeners in musical sounds themselves is at best a metaphorical connection.

15 When music was first composed directly into a concrete form in France in the late nineteen-forties using magnetic tape as a medium, it was called by the French term *musique concrète*. It was created by recording sounds onto tape and then manipulating them using electronic equipment, often transforming them to the point where the original sounds where no longer recognisable. Since this term, despite its broad potential, is so associated with those particular avant-garde tape experiments in post-war Europe, and is so often presumed only really to pertain to the institutionalised, so-called 'serious music' varieties that succeeded it, I'm using the term translated to English to refer to any music that exists in a concrete medium such as tape, vinyl, CD or mp3. Hit singles are concrete music because they're recorded in a studio and presented on a concrete medium, but calling them *musique concrète* would raise too many eyebrows.

16 Besides, strictly speaking, any music that differs *in time*

during a performance could be said to be flexible, including recorded music. We could think of 'the point of performance' as an infinitely small, specific instant in time, and if the values in a musical recording differ across any stretch of time at all then the music is still differing between at least two points of performance and so is flexible. In fact, even if the music repeats, it's still differing (values) across (a variable of) time because it appears at a different position in time. Thus when considering concrete music, we might not take into account music's temporal structure of differing at the point of performance – or put simply, its flexibility within a time range. In further discussions to come in Part 2, it can generally be assumed that infinitely specific concrete events are nevertheless still subject to a continuous variable or locus of temporal duration, i.e. that they still endure in time and have a duration (albeit a relatively limited one).

17 Not to mention something more bizarre, like an instrument that only plays at high values of a speed variable, and so can only play fast music.

18 Returning to the earlier example of monastic chant: if we were using language conventionally, we'd probably say that the liturgical chants were 'sung in different styles' from monastery to monastery, because we conventionally think of specific notes changing from performance to performance when we imagine the internal differences to expect within the concept of 'style'. Again, this shows the tenaciousness of such limited conceptions of stylistic possibility.

Part 2: Welcome to Music Space

19 John Cage, *Silence: Lectures and Writings* (1968), p. 9. Cage hyphenated 'sound' and 'space' in the original. In modern maths and science, particular spaces are rarely hyphenated with their qualifying terms in this way. I've omitted the hyphen for the sake of continuity with my term 'music space'

and subsequent similar terms, which loosely derive from these usages.

20   In a later essay, Cage reduced the number of characteristics to four: 'pitch, timbre, loudness, and duration', omitting 'morphology' ('Forerunners of Modern Music' in Cage, *Silence*, p. 63)

21   Ibid., p. 9.

22   This example was suggested by a composition by Peter Ablinger, *Voices and Piano*, which explores this concept by setting recordings of speech to a piano accompaniment that approximates the sonic qualities of that speech in various ways.

23   Having said this, in many cases a tape recorder unintentionally records the sound of its own mechanical operation onto the tape, stamping all its recordings with a specific and usually relatively quiet signature drone.

24   Similarly, by using dimensional analysis in maths and classical physics, all physical quantities can be 'broken down' into variables of mass, length, time, electric charge or current and temperature, related in different ways to make up other variables such as speed, force, electrical resistance etc.

25   Time can be specified in music a number of different ways, but even when it isn't specified at all (as is the case with a musical instrument), actualised music still relies on a 'backdrop' of time to make a sound, since a sound can't be made in zero seconds.

In a similar way, music can't technically be reduced to amplitude and time, because music requires an atmosphere (with mass) to make a sound. Composers could incorporate this as a musical variable by controlling an atmosphere through which the sound waves propagate, adjusting proportions of various gasses in it before or during the performance. This can have an effect on pitch – higher concentrations of carbon dioxide can cause lower pitches, for example. If the atmosphere to be adjusted were the natural ambient atmosphere in which any listeners reside, they would of course have to wear breathing apparatus. Until this becomes a regular musical practice – and because its effects can be reasonably and far more safely approximated using electronic equipment – it's sufficient to assume that the medium for music's sound waves will be the usual air.

26 A much more detailed introduction to phase spaces, their geometrical properties and their role in giving rise to different forms can be found in Manuel DeLanda, *Intensive Science and Virtual Philosophy* (2002).

27 It would be correct to say that this two-dimensional identity for the pendulum only partially constitutes the pendulum as it exists *in actuality*. It is an abstraction. As they actually exist in the universe, of course, every pendulum does have a colour and a location and other values for any other variables. A phase space cannot be constructed that would be true to all the possible attributes of the pendulum and all the variations thereof, because there is no absolute frame of reference for that full, actual, concrete truth other than that of the universe itself.

28 'The Future of Music: Credo', in Cage, *Silence*, p. 3.

29 Because of music space's ability to recognise any and all possible musical variables (to the point of infinite concreteness), music space cannot ultimately be distinguished from the universe itself. Composers cannot use composing systems that can constitute infinitely concrete performance events, their systems will always recognise less than an infinite number of variables. Composing systems (composers) can't constitute music with an infinite concreteness unless they are in complete control of the universe itself.

30 We can do even more bizarre things with musical objects. We

can imagine musical objects that break the known laws of physics, even if for obvious reasons we can't actually perform them within the physical universe. Recall the example of Performer A and Performer B from Part 1, where Performer B was asked to produced high-pitched sound if Performer A was producing low-pitched sound and vice versa, but imagine that Performer A has to be on Earth and Performer B has to be on Mars (never mind how s/he got there). Now imagine that they are given further instructions: Performer A is to vary the pitch of the sound they're producing at least once every minute, and Performer B is to respond appropriately to Performer A's pitch values within ten seconds. Light takes an average of forty minutes to travel from Earth to Mars, so Performer B cannot comply with the rules of the music unless the performers can somehow break the known rules (physical laws) of the universe and send or receive information from Earth faster than the speed of light. This musical work could not exist properly in the physical reality of our universe, but it can be described in abstract music space. Even if cosmologists haven't yet settled what the fundamental constants of the universe (such as the speed of light) are and how they're related yet, it appears that the universe is a constrained system. As such it can be thought of as a musical object that can't properly constitute such performance events in the same way that one speaker can't produce stereo effects. This illustrates once again how any musical objects we know are abstracted from the behaviour of our actual, physical universe.

31 This is a 'net' increase, or an average, overall increase, because since musical objects can be given different ranges of values across a number of variables, there is no single dimension through which music is specified. Two musical objects may both be equally specified by the same amount of degrees of freedom, but they may have a structure of

different variables, and thus a different dimensionality.

32 Technically speaking this space would be discrete, as we would only be able to jump between each sampled performance in its given entirety. With a little imagination (i.e. a little dequantisation), however, it can become a more continuous space, with the areas 'in between' each sampled performance representing various notional amalgamations of elements in the original performances.

33 This same applies to the sounds of our lives, of course, prior to a certain specific concept of 'music'.

Part 3: Aesthetics and Music Space

34 It's even possible that the speed of our brains could one day be artificially increased so that we can come to appreciate much of what to our unaided ears sounds like white noise. For the moment however, I think it's fair to say that the musical possibilities of human music space are quite ample.

35 J.J. Gibson, *The Senses Considered as Perceptual Systems* (1966), p. 285, via Eric Clarke, *Ways of Listening* (2005), pp. 36-37.

36 J. J. Gibson, *The Ecological Approach to Visual Perception* (1979), p. 122.

37 Eric F. Clarke, *Ways of Listening: An Ecological Approach to the Perception of Musical Meaning* (2005), p. 37.

38 Ibid., p. 47.

39 Ibid., pp. 37-8.

40 Ibid., p. 38.

41 Of course in reality, musical needs are rarely so basic, even if we're not explicitly aware of them – there are likely to be many musical styles we might not have wanted to dance to, perhaps for sensual reasons (e.g. it being too loud or too soft for us), physical reasons (e.g. it being too slow or two fast for us) or socio-cultural reasons (e.g. its having negative associations with certain groups of people and their ideologies).

42 Ibid., p. 37.

43   These square brackets are intended to suggest an editor inserting a qualifying term that a writer had, deliberately and/or mistakenly, merely left implied.

44   Some commentators have called this music 'hauntology' after a concept in the French philosopher Jacques Derrida's book *Specters of Marx* (1993) and in recognition of its 'haunting', 'ghostly' qualities. The term 'hauntology' isn't as widely known as much of the music is, and for many people it refers to a certain subset of this music concerned with representing images of British film and television music from the nineteen-sixties and -seventies, though I'd suggest that the term can be more widely applied to different musical styles and geographies. Notable artists in this field might include Boards of Canada, Ariel Pink, James Ferraro, Rangers, Matrix Metals, Philip Jeck, the Caretaker and William Basinski, while the composers on the Ghost Box record label, who first prompted Mark Fisher and Simon Reynolds to apply the word 'hauntology', focus on British film and television music of the mid-twentieth century. Far more artists can be thought of as hauntologically inclined to a lesser extent, and hauntology as a whole is arguably one of the prevailing aesthetic trends of the last decade, with examples spanning across many art fordms, even high street fashion. See my blogpost on the subject, 'Hauntology: The Past Inside the Present', http://rougesfoam.blogspot.com/2009/10/hauntology-past-inside-present.html.

45   Note that the word 'radical' historically refers to a root. This is exactly how alien genres are radical.

46   Such a statement may seem outrageous today, when millions of people are still without access to clean drinking water, but in July 2010 broadband internet access became a legal right in Finland, a highly developed nation. Many such developed nations are increasingly seeing internet access as part of the infrastructure they provide, along with roads, waste and

water. If developing nations come to cater for these latter, more fundamental rights in the future, it's reasonable to assume that the internet (or something like it) will be internationally and universally accessible as a right in the more distant future. This right of access may even extend to the provision of the necessary hardware. Of course, economic policies tending towards privatisation (i.e. neoliberalism) will delay and even prevent such developments.

47   Of course, this assumes a degree of social and political freedom that has not yet been universally won, and assumes moreover that societies will accept the advance of technology into their lives and living spaces, on whatever terms.

Epilogue: Into the Future

48   Fact magazine recently voted his second album, 2007's *Untrue*, the greatest of its decade. For more on the aesthetics of Burial's music, see my blogpost 'The Premature Burial: Burial the Pallbearer vs Burial the Innovator', http://rougesfoam.blogspot.com/2009/12/premature-burial-burial-pallbearer-vs.html.

Appendix: Alan Lomax's Cantometrics System

49   Alan Lomax, *Folk Song Style and Culture* (1968), p. 34.

50   Ibid., p. 35.

51   Ibid., p. 75.

52   Ibid., p. viii.

53   Ibid., p. 6.

54   Summarised from ibid., pp. 38-74.

Bibliography / Referenced Texts / Further Reading

Attali, Jacques. (1985) *Noise: The Political Economy of Music* (Trans. Brian Massumi). Minneapolis: University of Minnesota Press.

Badiou, Alain. (2005) *Being and Event* (Trans. Oliver Feltham). New York, London: Continuum

Badiou, Alain. (2005) *Infinite Thought*. New York, London: Continuum.

Badiou, Alain. (2009) *Logics of Worlds: Being and Event II* (Trans. Alberto Toscano). New York, London: Continuum.

Barlowe, Wayne Douglas. (1979) *Barlowe's Guide to Extraterrestrials*. New York: F. & S. Publications.

Barlowe, Wayne Douglas. (1990) *Expedition: Being an Account in Words and Artwork of the 2358 A. D. Voyage to Darwin IV*. New York: Workman Publishing.

Bernstein, Leonard. (1968) 'The Infinite Variety of Music' in *The Infinite Variety of Music*, p. 29-47. London: Weidenfeld & Nicolson.

Blacking, John. (1976) *How Musical is Man?* London: Faber and Faber.

Busoni, Ferruccio. (1911) *Sketch of a New Esthetic of Music* (Trans. Theodore Baker). New York: G Schirmer.

Cage, John. (1968) *Silence: Lectures and Writings*. New York, London: Marion Boyars.

Clarke, Eric. (2005) *Ways of Listening: An Ecological Approach to the Perception of Musical Meaning*. New York: Oxford University Press.

Cohen, Jack and Ian Stewart. (2002) *Evolving the Alien*. London: Ebury.

Colebrook, Claire. (2006) *Deleuze: A Guide for the Perplexed*. New York, London: Continuum.

Cox, Christoph and Daniel Warner (eds.). (2004) *Audio Culture:*

Readings in Modern Music. New York, London: Continuum.

DeLanda, Manuel. (1998) 'Deleuze, Diagrams, and the Genesis of Form' in *Any (Diagram Work: Data Mechanics for a Topological Age)* 23, pp. 30-34.

DeLanda, Manuel. (2002) *Intensive Science and Virtual Philosophy.* New York, London: Continuum.

Deleuze, Gilles. (2004) *Difference and Repetition* (Trans. Paul Patton). New York, London: Continuum.

Deleuze, Gilles. (2006) *Foucault* (Trans. Seán Hand). New York, London: Continuum.

Deleuze, Gilles and Félix Guattari. (1987) *A Thousand Plateaus* (Trans. Brian Massumi). New York, London: Continuum.

Deleuze, Gilles and Félix Guattari. (1994) *What is Philosophy?* (Trans. Hugh Tomlinson and Graham Burchill). New York, London: Verso.

Demers, Joanna. (2010) *Listening Through the Noise: The Aesthetics of Experimental Electronic Music.* New York: Oxford University Press.

DeNora, Tia. (2000) *Music in Everyday Life.* Cambridge: Cambridge University Press.

Derrida, Jacques. (1994) *Specters of Marx* (Trans. Peggy Kamuf). New York, Abingdon: Routledge.

Dixon, Dougal. (1981) *After Man: A Zoology of the Future.* New York: St. Martin's Press.

Duvignaud, Jean. (1972) *The Sociology of Art* (Trans. Timothy Wilson). London: Paladin.

Everett, Brian. (2006) *The Cambridge Dictionary of Statistics.* Cambridge: Cambridge University Press.

Fisher, Mark. (2009) *Capitalist Realism: Is There No Alternative?* Winchester, UK: O Books.

Fürniss, Susanne. (2006) 'Aka Polyphony: Music, Theory, Back and Forth' in Michael Tenzer (ed.), *Analytical Studies in World Music*, pp. 163-204. New York: Oxford University Press.

Gibson, James J. (1966) *The Senses Considered as Perceptual Systems.*

Boston: Houghton Mifflin.

Gibson, James J. (1979) *The Ecological Approach to Visual Perception*. Dallas, London: Houghton Mifflin.

Gillespie, Sam. (2008) *The Mathematics of Novelty: Badiou's Minimalist Metaphysics*. Melborune: re.press.

Goehr, Lydia. (1992) *The Imaginary Museum of Musical Works: An Essay in the Philosophy of Music*. Oxford: Clarendon.

Griffiths, Paul. (2011) *Modern Music and After*, third edition. New York: Oxford University Publications.

Hallward, Peter. (2003) *Badiou: A Subject to Truth*. Minneapolis, London: University of Minnesota Press.

Hallward, Peter. (2006) *Out of This World: Deleuze and the Philosophy of Creation*. New York, London: Verso.

Harper, Adam. (2009) 'Loving Wonky', at the *Rouge's Foam* blog, http://rougesfoam.blogspot.com/2009/06/loving-wonky.html

Harper, Adam. (2009) 'Hauntology: The Past Inside the Present', at the *Rouge's Foam* blog, http://rougesfoam.blogspot.com /2009/10/hauntology-past-inside-present.html.

Harper, Adam. (2009) 'The Premature Burial: Burial the Pallbearer vs Burial the Innovator', at the *Rouge's Foam* blog, http://rougesfoam.blogspot.com/2009/12/premature-burial-burial-pallbearer-vs.html.

Harper, Adam. (2010) 'Out of the Mould, the New', at the *Rouge's Foam* blog, http://rougesfoam.blogspot.com/2010/03/out-of-mould-new.html.

Harper, Adam. (2011) 'Always Read the Label: Night Slugs', at the *Rouge's Foam* blog, http://rougesfoam.blogspot .com/2011/01/artl-night-slugs.html.

Hatherley, Owen. (2008) *Militant Modernism*. Winchester, UK: O Books.

Lomax, Alan. (1968) *Folk Song Style and Culture*. New Brunswick and London: Transaction Publishers.

Lomax, Alan. (2005) *Selected Writings 1934-1997* (ed. Ronald D. Cohen). New York, London: Routledge.

Meyer, Leonard B. (1967) *Music, the Arts and Ideas: Patterns and Predictions in Twentieth-Century Culture*. Chicago, London: University of Chicago Press.

Nattiez, Jean-Jacques. (1990) *Music and Discourse: Toward a Semiology of Music* (Trans. Carolyn Abbate). Princeton, NJ: Princeton University Press.

Nicolis, Grégoire and Ilya Prigogine. (1989) *Exploring Complexity: An Introduction*. New York: W. H. Freeman and Company.

Nyman, Michael. (1999) *Experimental Music: Cage and Beyond*, second edition. Cambridge: Cambridge University Press.

Partch, Harry. (1974) *Genesis of a Music*, second edition. New York: Da Capo Press.

Partch, Harry. (1990) *Bitter Music: Collected Journals, Essays, Introductions, and Librettos*. Urbana: University of Illinois Press.

Pierce, John R. (1980) *An Introduction to Information Theory: Symbols, Signals and Noise*, second edition. New York: Dover.

Porkess, Roger. (2004) *Collins Dictionary of Statistics*. Glasgow: HarperCollins.

Rancière, Jacques. (2004) *The Politics of Aesthetics* (Trans. Gabriel Rockhill). New York and London: Continuum.

Reynolds, Simon. (2008) *Energy Flash: A Journey Through Rave Music and Culture*, second edition. London: Picador.

Roads, Curtis. (2001) *Microsound*. Cambridge, Mass., London: MIT Press.

Sauer, Theresa. (2009) *Notations 21*. New York: Mark Batty.

Shaviro, Steven. (2009) *Without Criteria: Kant, Whitehead, Deleuze, and Aesthetics*. Cambridge, Mass., London: MIT Press.

Small, Christopher. (1998) *Musicking: The Meanings of Performing and Listening*. Hanover: University Press of New England.

Théberge, Paul. (1997) *Any Sound You Can Imagine: Making Music, Consuming Technology*. Hanover, London: Wesleyan University Press.

Todd, Stephen and William Latham. (1992) *Evolutionary Art and*

Computers. San Diego and London: Academic Press.

Toop, David. (1995) *Ocean of Sound: Aether Talk, Ambient Sound and Imaginary Worlds*. London: Serpent's Tail.

Toop, David. (2004) *Haunted Weather: Music, Silence and Memory*. London: Serpent's Tail.

Walker, Helen M. (1940) 'Degrees of Freedom' in *Journal of Educational Psychology* 31 (4). pp. 253-269.

Contemporary culture has eliminated both the concept of the public and the figure of the intellectual. Former public spaces – both physical and cultural – are now either derelict or colonized by advertising. A cretinous anti-intellectualism presides, cheerled by expensively educated hacks in the pay of multinational corporations who reassure their bored readers that there is no need to rouse themselves from their interpassive stupor. The informal censorship internalized and propagated by the cultural workers of late capitalism generates a banal conformity that the propaganda chiefs of Stalinism could only ever have dreamt of imposing. Zer0 Books knows that another kind of discourse – intellectual without being academic, popular without being populist – is not only possible: it is already flourishing, in the regions beyond the striplit malls of so-called mass media and the neurotically bureaucratic halls of the academy. Zer0 is committed to the idea of publishing as a making public of the intellectual. It is convinced that in the unthinking, blandly consensual culture in which we live, critical and engaged theoretical reflection is more important than ever before.